EXIN CLOUD Computing Foundation

Workbook

Johannes W. van den Bent
Martine van der Steeg

Edition: May 2012

CLOUD COMPUTING
FOUNDATION

Colophon

Title	EXIN CLOUD Computing Foundation – Workbook
Authors	Johannes W. van den Bent Martine van der Steeg
Editor	Eline Kleijer (EXIN)
Publisher	Van Haren Publishing
ISBN Hardcopy	978 94 018 0252 9
ISBN eBook	978 90 820388 7 3
Edition	October 2015

Table of contents

Introduction

Cloud Computing is about providing IT related services through the Internet. Cloud Computing allows flexible IT solutions to support the business, based on clear service arrangements.

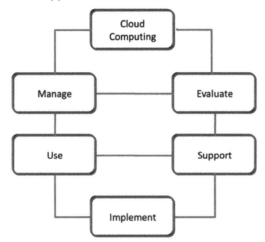

This workbook will help you prepare for the EXIN Cloud Computing Foundation exam and provides you with an overview of Cloud Computing and its relationship with other areas of Information management. Topics discussed are the fundamental concepts of Cloud Computing like architecture, design, and deployment models of Cloud Computing, and how it can be employed by different types of organizations. The exam consists of 40 multiple choice questions. The exam requirements are specified at the beginning of each chapter, and the weight of the different exam topics is expressed as a percentage of the total.

Target audience

Everyone who wishes to prepare for the EXIN Cloud Computing Foundation exam, and everyone interested in the basics of information processing in the Cloud.

Exam preparation

To help prepare for the exam, you can download the EXIN Cloud Computing Sample Exam and Preparation Guide from the EXIN website (www.exin.com) for free. In this workbook you will find several *"get it"* questions to help increase your knowledge about Cloud Computing. You will find these questions at the end of each chapter. Additionally you are provided with an overview of terms with which you should be familiar.

The principles of Cloud Computing: exam specifications

After reading chapter 1, you will understand the principles of Cloud Computing (30%).

1.1 The concept of Cloud Computing (5%)

You can:

1.1.1 Explain what Cloud Computing is

1.1.2 Compare the main Deployment Models for Cloud Computing (Private, Public, Community and Hybrid Cloud)

1.1.3 Describe the main Service Models for Cloud Computing (SaaS, PaaS and IaaS)

1.2 The evolution of Cloud Computing (10%)

You can:

1.2.1 Describe the main concepts from which Cloud Computing developed

1.2.2 Explain the role of network and servers in Cloud Computing

1.2.3 Describe the role of the Internet in Cloud Computing

1.2.4 Explain the role of Virtualization in Cloud Computing

1.2.5 Describe the role of managed services in Cloud Computing

1.3 Cloud Computing architectures (10%)

You can:

1.3.1 Explain the difference between a single purpose and multipurpose architecture

1.3.2 Describe the Service Oriented Architecture

1.4 Benefits and limitations of Cloud Computing (5%)

You can:

1.4.1 Identify the main drivers for Cloud Computing

1.4.2 Identify the main limitations of Cloud Computing

1. The principles of Cloud Computing

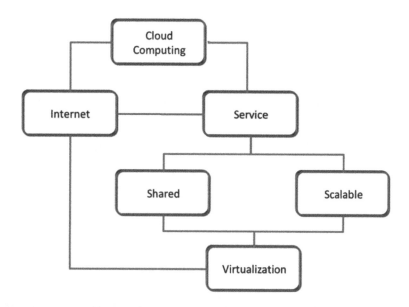

"Cloud Computing, method of running application software and storing related data in central computer systems and providing customers or other users access to them through the Internet".

Encyclopaedia Britannica (www.britannica.com, as viewed on 10-09-2015)

1.1 The concept of Cloud Computing

To understand the concept of Cloud Computing we need to know how it has evolved. But first we need to have a look at another definition. According to the American National Institute of Standards and Technology (NIST):

"Cloud Computing is a model for enabling ubiquitous, convenient, on-demand network access to a shared pool of configurable computing resources (e.g., networks, servers, storage, applications, and services) that can be rapidly provisioned and released with minimal management effort or service provider interaction."

NIST Special Publication 800-145 (September 2011)

At the present date this definition has been approved or adopted by many organizations in the industry, for example by:

- The International Standards Organization (ISO); reference: ISO/IEC 17788:2014 Information technology -- Cloud computing -- Overview and vocabulary

> *"Cloud Computing is a paradigm for enabling network access to a scalable and elastic pool of shareable physical or virtual resources with self-service provisioning and administration on-demand."*
>
> ISO/IEC 17788:2014 (October 2014)

- The International Telecommunication Union (ITU); reference: Recommendation ITU-T Y.3500 Information technology -- Cloud computing -- Overview and vocabulary (2014)
- The Cloud Industry Forum (CIF); reference: Paper five Cloud Definitions, Deployment Considerations & Diversity (2012)

For this workbook we will use the NIST definition as a basis. NIST states that there are "five essential characteristics, three service models, and four deployment models." We will discuss the five characteristics first.

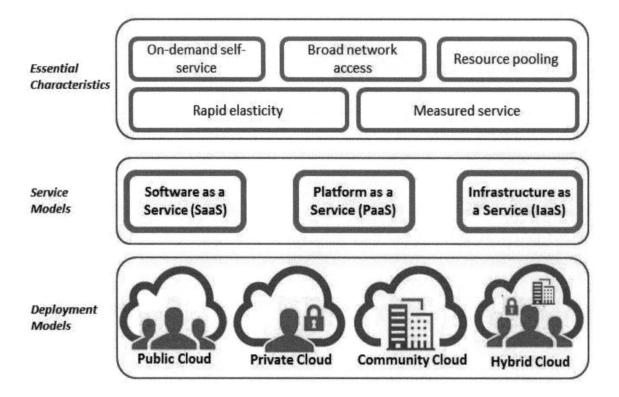

1.1.1 Five Cloud characteristics

- *On-demand self-service*; within an existing contract, a user/customer can for example add new services, storage space or computing power without a formal request for change.
- *Broad network access*; this is what Microsoft's Bill Gates envisioned in the late nineties: "any time, any place, and any device". And of course also with enough bandwidth.
- *Resource pooling*; in the industry, this characteristic is also known as *Multi-tenancy*. Many users/customers share a varied type and level of resources.
- *Rapid elasticity*; this characteristic has to do with the fundamental Cloud aspects of flexibility and scalability. For example, web shops need a standard amount of transaction ability during the year, but need to peak around Christmas. Of course they do not want to pay for this peak ability during the rest of the year.
- *Measured service*; this means monitored, controlled, and reported services. This characteristic enables a pay-per-use service model. It has similarities to the mobile telephone concept of service bundles, where you pay a standard subscription for basic levels, and pay extra for additional service without changing the contract.

The ISO/IEC 17788 standard recognizes a sixth characteristic:
- *Multi-tenancy;* A feature where physical or virtual resources are allocated in such a way that multiple tenants and their computations and data are isolated from and inaccessible to one another. Typically, and within the context of multi-tenancy, the group of cloud service users that form a tenant will all belong to the same cloud service customer organization. There might be cases where the group of cloud service users involves users from multiple different cloud service customers, particularly in the case of Public Cloud and Community Cloud deployments. However, a given cloud service customer organization might have many different tenancies with a single cloud service provider representing different groups within the organization.

NIST furthermore defines four Deployment models: Private Cloud, Community Cloud, Public Cloud and Hybrid Cloud, and three main Service Models: Infrastructure as a Service (IaaS), Platform as a Service (PaaS) and Software as a Service (SaaS). The deployment models will be discussed in the next paragraph, and the three Service models will be discussed in paragraph 1.1.3.

1.1.2 The main Cloud Deployment Models

It is tempting to talk about "the Cloud" as one environment. However, studying all Cloud phenomena must lead to the conclusion that there are many different Clouds. For a normal end-user of web based services like social media, webmail, online storage, collaboration software, blogs, video calling and so on, there seems to be only one Cloud, the World Wide Web. But for enterprises, public sector organizations and non-government organizations it is more of a Cloudy sky. Most own their own IT infrastructure, buy IT services from Service Providers and use several web services. For example, an organization's email infrastructure typically consists of (a number of) Exchange servers on which every employee has their own ID and mailbox, agenda and corporate contact list. However, most employees will also have access to a webmail account connecting them to the corporate mail server through the Internet. In this case there obviously is a Private and a Public aspect.

In the industry there are four types of Cloud Deployment Models that are generally accepted; most prominently by the American National Institute of Standards and Technology (NIST).

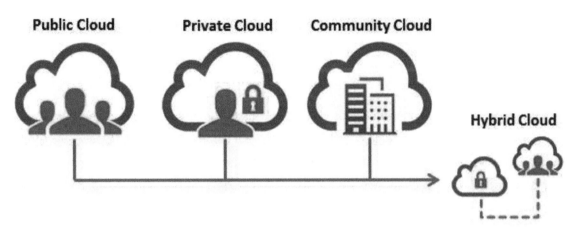

The Private Cloud

The main characteristic of a Private Cloud is that it resides on a private network that runs on (part of) a data center. The data center may be owned, managed and run by either the organization itself, a third party or a combination of the two. Services are delivered to the different parts of the organization; i.e., its business units and internal departments like human resources and finance. The goal is to support the organization's business objectives in an economic sound way, but more important in a secure way. A Private Cloud solution is usually chosen when there is a need to comply with external regulations and legislation like the Sarbanes-Oxley (SOX) Act causing the need for a high degree of governance.

The downside of this solution is that there is still a high degree of total cost of ownership (TCO). An organization needs to consider if it really needs access at any time, from any place and from any device; i.e., a Cloud or just a shared service center. All types of Cloud have the before mentioned five characteristics; if not the services are just classical examples of hosting or ASP.

The Public Cloud

A Public Cloud is a more compelling example of what is intended with Cloud Computing, namely the delivery of off-site services over the Internet. Key characteristics are the sharing of resources, thus lowering TCO and high flexibility and scalability of capacity, also called Elasticity. The downside of this sharing principle of multi-tenancy is a lower level of security and privacy making it more difficult to comply with different types of international legislation. Sharing basic infrastructure like storage, data base servers or applications can all cause (data) security and privacy issues.

For example when a multinational chain of retail stores with their head office in the Netherlands decided to migrate their Office applications to the Google Apps for business platform, their main requirement was that their data would be stored on a data center within the European Union.

For most private users or the main public these concerns are less relevant or not appreciated. For this target group the Cloud is Facebook, Twitter, Skype, Flickr, Webmail and all the other examples of Internet based offerings that make life more productive or fun.

The Community Cloud

The Community Cloud has many similarities with the Private Cloud in that it delivers services to a specific group of organizations and/or individuals that share a common goal. Examples are regional or national educational or research institutes, community centers or even commercial organizations wishing to share very high security facilities for transaction processing like stock exchange trading companies.

The main goal for creating a Community Cloud is the ease of sharing data and platforms and applications which otherwise would be too expensive to purchase like research equipment. Another goal of sharing Cloud facilities with your own community may be to reduce costs, improve performance and privacy and security without raising TCO in a significant way. Some specific advantages could not easily be gained by running your own local computing facilities: 24/7 access and support, shared service and support contracts and the economics of scale.

The Hybrid Cloud

Putting it in a simple way, a Hybrid Cloud is a mix of the above models. It combines several private and public Cloud solutions from several providers into one IT infrastructure. In this model a clear choice will have to be made what to buy where. Choosing specific services for either Private or Public Cloud suitability is balancing security, privacy and compliance versus price.

Let us look at an example. A large multinational made the choice to go "the Hybrid way". The mission critical logistics and enterprise resource planning (ERP) systems run on a Private Cloud solution, while the common office applications are fulfilled by the Google Apps for business solution. This brings savings of many million dollars per annum and does not compromise the integrity of the core business services.

Another example could be the way insurance companies work with insurance agents. There is a lot of interaction between the two sides, but the company's and agents infrastructures can and will not be integrated in the traditional way. In this scenario a Public Cloud extension could build a bridge between the two.

1.1.3 Service Models for Cloud Computing

There are many types of Cloud services like webmail, hosted Exchange, online storage, online backup, social media, etc. All these services can be grouped under three main Cloud service models: Software as a Service (SaaS), Platform as a Service (PaaS) and Infrastructure as a Service (IaaS). SPI is an acronym for the most common Cloud Computing service models. In this paragraph we will briefly describe these three models.

Software as a service (SaaS)

This is the most common type of Cloud service. SaaS is a software delivery methodology that provides licensed multi-tenant access to software and its functions remotely as a Web-based service. SaaS is a break with tradition that organizations buy or develop their own business applications and run and manage them on their own IT Infrastructure. Application hosting by third parties goes back to the mainframe days, and came into maturity with the ASP industry that emerged in the early 2000's. SaaS essentially extends the idea of the ASP model. Many types of SaaS services were developed from ASP solutions, e.g., application hosting, pay per license, emulation, terminal services, etc., into Cloud solutions, e.g., multi-tenancy, pay-per-use, web based interfaces, elastic, etc.

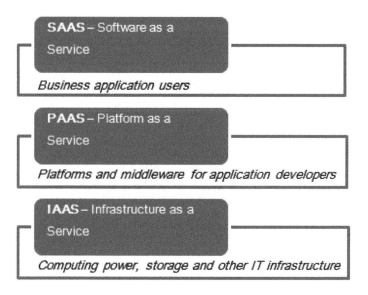

Typical examples of SaaS solutions are:
- CRM
- HR
- ERP
- Billing and invoicing
- Web Hosting
- E-commerce
- Transaction processing
- Online collaboration

and other business processes

<u>Key characteristics:</u>

- software hosted offsite
- software on demand
- software package
- no modification of the software
- plug-in software: external software used with internal applications (Hybrid Cloud)
- vendor with advanced technical knowledge
- user entangled with vendor

The key benefits are that the customer does not need to worry about the development and management of these applications. The provider is responsible for updates and managing licenses, and most service management parameters like scalability, availability, maintenance and service continuity. A customer pays by means of a subscription or pay-per-use model.

Sub-types, or maybe simply other names for SaaS, are "software on demand," "hosted services" and "application service provisioning." DBaaS (Database as a Service) has emerged as a sub-variety of SaaS.

Platform as a Service (PaaS)

Not owning a computer platform, but being able to use it "on demand" can save costs in ownership, management and maintenance. In a typical software development environment platforms are used for the time the project runs, and a new project often has other or newer platform requirements.

During some stages of the development process, e.g., testing, there often is a need for an up-scaled environment to simulate a production environment. PaaS services can offer this on-demand scalability.

There are several types of PaaS:

Public PaaS: It is derived from Software as a Service (SaaS) and is situated in Cloud Computing between SaaS and Infrastructure as a Service (IaaS).

Private PaaS: Typically it can be downloaded and installed either on a company's on-premises infrastructure, or more often in a public cloud. Once the software is installed on one or more machines, the private PaaS arranges the application and database components into a single hosting platform.

Hybrid PaaS: It is able to "register" multiple, distinct cloud infrastructures as independent pools and merge those identifiably different pools into a single resource pool. This leads to resource normalization while still preserving identity of origin.

Mobile PaaS: mPaaS provides development capabilities for mobile app designers and developers.

Open PaaS: It does not include hosting, but rather it provides open source software allowing a PaaS provider to run applications in an open source environment.

PaaS for Rapid Development: Enterprise Public Cloud Platforms for Rapid Developers is defined by Forrester Research as an emerging trend.

The most common variants of PaaS are:
-   Software development environment; a customer can develop an application without having to buy a dedicated development environment, and without having to configure and manage the underlying infrastructure components like hardware, middleware and the different software layers. Microsoft Azure and the Google App engine are examples of such a service.
-   Hosting environment for applications; this service only consists of services at the hosting level like security and on-demand scalability.
-   Online storage; Cloud solutions, because of their architecture with Storage Area Network (SAN) servers, not only offer online storage but also extremely rapid data exchange between instances of online storage.

Key characteristics:
-   Mostly used for remote application development
-   Remote application support
-   Platform may have special features
-   Low development costs

Some examples of PaaS service providers are Force.com, the first PaaS provider, Google with its App Engine and smaller players like Heroku.

Infrastructure as a Service (IaaS)

IaaS provides access to computing resources in a virtualized environment, "the Cloud", across a public connection, usually the internet. The definition includes such offerings as virtual server space, network connections, bandwidth, IP addresses and load balancers. Physically, the pool of hardware resource is pulled from a multitude of servers and networks usually distributed across numerous data centers, all of which the cloud provider is responsible for maintaining. The client, on the other hand, is given access to the virtualized components in order to build their own IT platforms.

IaaS services are sold by so called hardware service providers from which a customer can rent physical or virtual hardware like storage, servers or Internet connectivity. Services are sold according to a utility computing service and billing model. The background of IaaS can be found in the merger between IT and Telecom infrastructure and services in the past decade.

Key characteristics:
- Dynamic scaling
- Desktop virtualization
- Policy-based services

Perhaps the best known provider of IaaS is Amazon with products like EC2 for processing power and S3 for storage. IaaS ERP software, among other things, is offered by SAP. Many of these on demand IaaS infrastructures are built on components from leading vendors like Cisco, HP, NetApp, and VMware.

With the IaaS model large enterprise like IT infrastructures and services come within the reach of smaller business like Small to Medium Enterprises/Businesses (SME/SMB).

Anything as a Service (XaaS)

Anything as a service, or XaaS, refers to the growing diversity of services available over the Internet via Cloud Computing as opposed to being provided locally, or on premises. Also known as everything as a service, anything as a service reflects the vast potential for on-demand cloud services and is already being heavily marketed and promoted by companies like VMware and HP.

Anything as a service derives the "X" in its XaaS acronym as a result of being a catch-all term for everything from storage as a service (SaaS) to Desktop as a Service (DaaS), Disaster Recovery as a Service (DRaaS), Network as a Service (NaaS), and even emerging services such as Marketing as a Service and Healthcare as a Service.

Occasionally, one can find approaches such as Backup as a Service (BaaS), Business Process as a Service (BPaaS), Container as a Service (CaaS), Communications as a Service (CaaS), Data as a Service (DaaS), Database as a Service (DBaaS), Identity as a Service (IDaaS), Monitoring as a Service (MaaS) and Security as a Service (SecaaS) and other. Depending on the point of view they can be classified within the classic three (IaaS, PaaS and SaaS).

Cloud service categories	Cloud capabilities types		
	Infrastructure	Platform	Application
Compute as a Service	X		
Communications as a Service		X	X
Data Storage as a Service	X	X	X
Infrastructure as a service	X		
Network as a Service	X	X	X
Platform as a Service		X	
Software as a Service			X

(Source: ISO/IEC 17788:2014)

1.2 How Cloud Computing evolved

Cloud Computing is often compared with the supply models of the electrical grid or water companies. Computing power from the tap, turn it on when you need it, and turn it off when you do not need it, only pay for use and for the connection to the supply.

This comparison between computing and common utilities was made as early as 1996 by Douglas Parkhill in his book "The Challenge of Computer Utility" (Parkhill, 1996). He stated that when the electrical grid was built it quickly replaced all the small private plants and providers. Large scale economics, in combination with security and safety won the day. This theme was discussed in more detail by Nicolas Carr in his book "The Big Switch: Rewiring the World, from Edison to Google" (Carr, 2008).

Historic timeline

A number of key factors have contributed to the present day existence of "the Cloud":
- the development of the Internet
- the move from Mainframe computing to the present day myriad of personal devices with connection to the Internet
- the development of computer networks

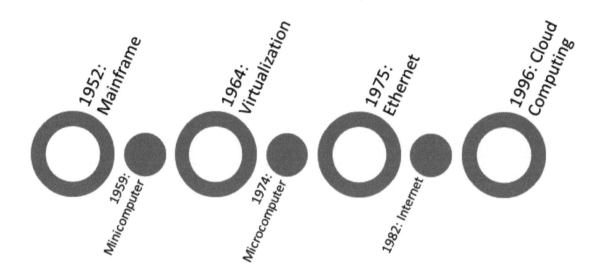

1.2.1 Networks, servers and all that stuff

The first mainframe computers were not connected to what we nowadays call a network. At first they had a point-to-point connection with a terminal. The first terminals did not even have a monitor.

When business applications started to run on mainframes, users got their own terminals, but these were not interconnected. All data processing and information sharing was done on the mainframe computer. When decentralized computing started to appear the first so-called mini computers were developed. The first generation of these decentralized computers with their own attached terminals was called mini computers (or sometimes front end processor). These decentralized computers were connected through local (LAN) or wide area (WAN) connections to the central mainframe computer.

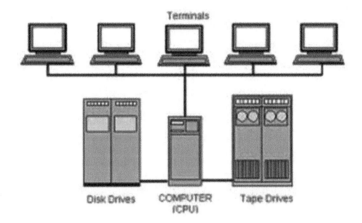

Terminals

Disk Drives   COMPUTER   Tape Drives
                (CPU)

When IBM started selling their first so-called microcomputer, the IBM PC, it was predicted that there would only be a need for a few of these per office, and most likely stand-alone.

We now know that almost immediately there came a need to connect these PC's to the central computers through a network. Instead of having a mainframe terminal plus a PC on your desk, you could have a PC connected to a network and access the mainframe with a terminal emulation program. Several network topologies were developed, many with their own protocol. The most commonly known are: Point-to-point, Bus, Star, Ring or circular, Mesh, Tree, Hybrid and Daisy chain.

The most common topology today is the star topology in combination with the TCP/IP protocol. It is important to realize that the so-called Transmission Control Protocol (TCP) / Internet protocol (IP) stack is the core protocol of the Internet. From PC's connected to the mainframe the next development was the client-server architecture. PC's were now able to connect to several different mini computers called servers, e.g., file servers, application servers, etc. With ever growing bandwidth and speed of the networks, server speed and capacity, and ever cheaper and smaller personal devices to connect to the networks we entered the age of the Internet and Application Hosting by application service providers (ASP). One of the present day variants of the Cloud service SaaS (Software as a Service) is a direct derivative of these ASP solutions.

1.2.2   The role of the Internet

On April 25, 1963 the American computer scientist J. C. R. Licklider, Director of Behavioral Sciences Command & Control Research at ARPA, the U. S. Department of Defense Advanced Research Projects Agency, sent a memo to his colleagues explaining his vision on a global network. The memo was called: *"Memorandum For Members and Affiliates of the Intergalactic Computer Network."* This vision was later realized in 1969 in the form of the ARPANET, the direct predecessor to the Internet. ARPANET was the world's first operational packet switching network, but designed for the armed forces of the USA, and therefore not (yet) public.

The original network protocol NCP was replaced by TCP/IP in 1983 and remains the leading protocol to the present day. Based on the address restriction of the Internet Protocol v4 the Internet layer has essentially to be replaced by IPv6 in the layer model. The remaining layers of this model remain relatively untouched, unless there are more addresses included in the application layer, as is the case with FTP.

The Internet is sometimes called the World Wide Web (WWW), but that is just the name of one of the many services that run on the Internet like FTP (data transfer) and SMTP (E-mail). To make the Internet accessible to everyone, first there needed to be two other developments: personal devices and network connectivity. These developments happened in parallel and started with terminals connected to a mainframe giving access to central computing facilities and applications.

1.2.3   Virtualization

Virtualization refers to the act of creating a virtual (rather than actual) version of something, including (but not limited to) a virtual computer hardware platform, operating system (OS), storage device or computer network resources. Virtualization began in the 1960s, as a method of logically dividing the system resources provided by mainframe computers between different applications.

In his book "Virtualization: A Manager's Guide" (Kuznetzky, 2011) Daniel Kuznetzky describes the earliest examples of virtualization: "The earliest form of application virtualization were developed by mainframe suppliers, such as IBM..." An example is the IBM VM/370 from 1972.
Since the 1990's, Windows has also become the center of virtualization developments by Microsoft, Citrix, VMware and others.

Kuznetzky recognizes six different types of virtualization (Kuznetzky 2011):

- Access virtualization — Allows access to any application from any device
- Application virtualization — Enables applications to run on many different operating systems and hardware platforms
- Processing virtualization — Makes one system seem like many, or many seem like one
- Network virtualization — Presents an artificial view of the network that differs from the physical reality
- Storage virtualization — Allows many systems to share the same storage devices, enables concealing the location of storage systems, and more

For the average Cloud user this means that hardware, applications and data can be located anywhere in the Cloud; we only need to access and use them.

Virtualization is the solution for integration of:

- High-speed computers
- Large storage capacity
- Internet

Key Features are:

- Virtualization multiplies the use of high performance computers.
- With today's modern processors there is a vast amount of processor availability. Virtualization puts extra capacity to use.
- Concept of the Cloud: virtualized operating environment & thin clients; Web-based delivery
- Multi-tenancy

1.2.4 Managed Services

Managed services are the practice of outsourcing day-to-day management responsibilities and functions as a strategic method for improving operations and cutting expenses. Having your services managed basically means that you turn IT services over to a third party. An old example, since mainframe days, is Application Hosting by an IT provider. In the late 1990's applications were actually offered by providers, meaning that they were no longer owned by the customer. This first example of shared managed services was delivered by ASP's (application service providers). Because of the bursting 'Internet bubble' in the early 2000's the ASP never became the big thing and slowly developed into one of the major Cloud service models SaaS.

In parallel with these managed services arose the need for a good service management framework. With the IBM so-called Redbooks (operation guides etc.) as a basis and the adoption of many industry best practices, the IT Infrastructure Library (ITIL®) framework for IT Service Management was developed in the early 1970's.

Key internal ITIL® processes for a Cloud data center include Availability management, Capacity management, Security management and Service continuity management. External processes include Service level management; maintaining, managing, reporting on and improving service levels sold to and agreed with the customer and Financial Management. The customer's own IT department can shift their focus from operational issues, they no longer having to worry about constant server updates and other maintenance issues, but this does not mean that the CIO can sit back in his chair.

The shift of focus will have to be in the direction of IT Governance. Key issues are:

- Performance; can the Cloud services support our business model, also when it is transforming?
- Compliance; do the services comply with our own national and international legislation?
- Contingency; what happens if the Cloud provider goes out of business?

How can a customer stay 'in the driver's seat'? It seems likely that there will be an increased need for audit models focusing on the IT Service Management processes and data center performance and compliance issues. Data centers with a history of platform and application hosting often use the following ISO/IEC audit standards and guidelines for their internal and external audit mechanisms. (Source: ISO.org and isaca.org)

- ISO 19011:2011; *Guidelines for auditing management systems*
- ISO/IEC 20000-1:2011; *Information technology -- Service management -- Part 1: Service management system requirements*
- ISO/IEC 20000-2:2012; *Information technology -- Service management -- Part 2: Guidance on the implementation of service management systems*
- ISO/IEC TR 20000-9:2015; *Information technology -- Service management -- Part 9: Guidance on the application of ISO/IEC 20000-1 to cloud services*
- ISO/IEC 27001:2013; *Information technology -- Security techniques -- Information security management systems -- Requirements*
- ISO/IEC 27002:2013; *Information technology -- Security techniques -- Code of practice for information security controls*
- ISO/IEC 27007:2011; *Information technology -- Security techniques -- Guidelines for information security management systems auditing*
- ISO/IEC DIS 27017; *Information technology -- Security techniques -- Code of practice for information security controls based on ISO/IEC 27002 for cloud services (under development)*
- ISO/IEC 27018:2014; *Information technology -- Security techniques -- Code of practice for protection of personally identifiable information (PII) in public clouds acting as PII processors*
- ISO/IEC CD 27036-4; *Information technology -- Information security for supplier relationships -- Part 4: Guidelines for security of Cloud services (under development)*
- ISO/IEC 24762:2008; *Information technology -- Security techniques -- Guidelines for information and communications technology disaster recovery services*

For customers of Cloud services good Governance practices will be of increasing importance and this will place more focus on the following international standards and frameworks for corporate governance of information technology:

- COBIT™ 5 - *Guidance for executive management to govern IT within the enterprise*
- ISO/IEC 38500:2015 - *Information technology -- Governance of IT for the organization*

Even now, the purchase of bare metal can be modelled in commercial cloud (for example, billing by usage or put another way, physical server billing by the hour). The result of this is that a bare metal server request with all the resources needed, and nothing more, can be delivered within a matter of hours.

In the end, the story is not finished here. The evolution of Cloud Computing has only just begun.

1.3 Cloud Computing architectures

Two key architectural principles apply to Cloud Computing, multipurpose architecture and multi-tenancy. In the past most architectures were proprietary and single purpose. Examples are accounting systems and storage of healthcare data. Key to Cloud Computing is that the infrastructure is multipurpose. An example could be a system on which data is not only stored, but also distributed over the Internet.

1.3.1 Multipurpose architecture

Virtualization is one of the key factors that contribute to this characteristic. Many different types of implementation can run on the same (type of) platform in a virtual environment. In this way it is easy to guarantee scalability to all customers. Re-installing a new dedicated virtual platform is much quicker and easier than (re-)installing a physical server.

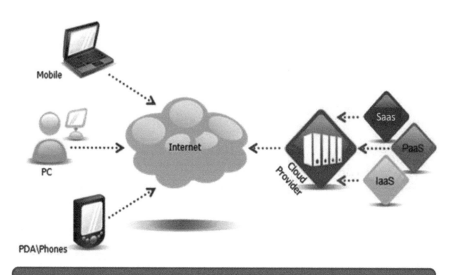

A new world for delivery of IT services

Key Characteristics:

- Multi-tiered (different tiers for Database, application and load balancing)
- Virtualization (server)
- Interoperable layers
- Open standards
- Portability

1.3.2 Multi-tenancy architecture

Multi-tenancy is an architecture in which a single instance of a software application serves multiple customers. Each customer is called a tenant. Tenants may be given the ability to customize some parts of the application, such as color of the user interface (UI) or business rules, but they cannot customize the application's code.

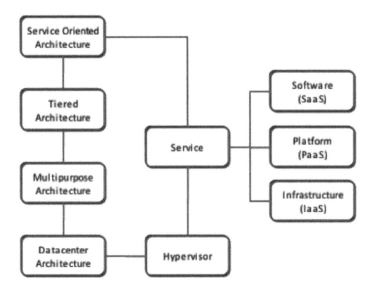

Multi-tenancy can be economical because software development and maintenance costs are shared. It can be contrasted with single-tenancy, an architecture in which each customer has their own software instance and may be given access to code. With a multi-tenancy architecture, the provider only has to make updates once. With a single-tenancy architecture, the provider has to touch multiple instances of the software in order to make updates.

In Cloud Computing, the meaning of multi-tenancy architecture has broadened because of new service models that take advantage of virtualization and remote access. A Software as a Service (SaaS) provider, for example, can run one instance of its application on one instance of a database and provide web access to multiple customers. In such a scenario, each tenant's data is isolated and remains invisible to other tenants.

In his article "Multi-Tenancy Misconceptions in Cloud Computing", Srinivasan Sundara Rajan states the business case for multi-tenancy: *"a large number of users, basically multi tenants, makes the Cloud platform most efficient in terms of usability of the application and 'Do More With Less Resources."* (Rajan 2011).

He also gives some examples of multi-tenant solutions:

- Salesforce.com: a SaaS-based CRM application for various businesses using common framework and multi tenancy model
- Microsoft Dynamics CRM Online offering
- Multi-tenancy IaaS/PaaS offerings from Amazon or IBM or Microsoft Azure

A key element of multi-tenancy is security. If security cannot be guaranteed on all levels of the infrastructure, from the basic infrastructure to the web interface, customers will be hesitant to adopt this model.

1.3.3 Service Oriented Architecture (SOA)

In his article 'The Cloud-SOA connection' (Krill, 2009) Paul Krill quotes Jerry Cuomo, CTO of IBM's WebSphere business. His question "Can we build a datacenter infrastructure on SOA principles?" is answered by Cuomo with: *"Yes, and that's the Cloud, so it's a service-oriented infrastructure,... It's taking that architectural principle of SOA and applying it to an infrastructure.'"*

The Open Group's SOA Work Group has come up with the following definition:

Service-Oriented Architecture (SOA) is an architectural style that supports service orientation.
Service orientation is a way of thinking in terms of services and service-based development and the outcomes of services.

> *A service:*
>
> - *is a logical representation of a repeatable business activity that has a specified outcome (e.g., check customer credit; provide weather data, consolidate drilling reports)*
> - *is self-contained*
> - *may be composed of other services*
> - *is a "black box" to consumers of the service*
>
> This definition of SOA was produced by the SOA Work Group's Definition of SOA project.
> ©the Open Group™

SOA is the instantiation of interoperability, portability and scalability. A service-oriented architecture is basically a collection of services that communicate with each other. This communication may be simply passing of data between two or more services or a jointly managed activity. Connecting these services in many cases involves Web services using XML.

Historically it goes back to the CORBA specification. One could say that there would be no Cloud without SOA.

1.4   Drivers and limitations of Cloud Computing

Cloud Computing is now evolving like never before, with companies of all shapes and sizes adapting to this new technology. Industry experts believe that this trend will only continue to grow and develop even further in the coming few years. While Cloud Computing is undoubtedly beneficial for mid-size to large companies, it is not without its downsides, especially for smaller businesses.

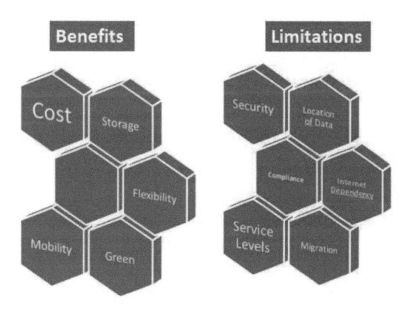

1.4.1 Main benefits of Cloud Computing

If used properly and to the extent necessary, working with data in the cloud can vastly benefit all types of businesses. Mentioned below are some of the advantages of this technology:

- **Reduced Cost**: because of the pay-per-use and/or subscription model organizations do not have to invest in IT infrastructure upfront. For Cloud providers costs are lower because of the economics of scale and the multi-tenancy principle; no 'floor space' is left unused.
- **Automated**: updates, security patches and backups are no longer a concern of the customer. No longer do IT personnel need to worry about keeping software up-to-date.
- **Flexibility**: Cloud Computing offers more flexibility than legacy IT services. Within an existing or standard contract a customer can change the 'Cloud mix' of services in a dynamic way to support business demands and requirements.
- **More Mobility**: data and applications can be accessed through the Internet from any type of smart computing device at anytime and anywhere.
- **Shared Resources**: customers share resources allowing smaller organizations to have access to corporate scale IT facilities, services and supporting services. Users belonging to one or more customers can work together in a shared project environment.
- **Agility and scalability**: enterprises can scale their IT infrastructure up or down 'on demand'.
- **Back to core business**: most types of start-up business do not need to own and operate IT.
- **More IT functionality for a lower price**: by sharing.

1.4.2 Main limitations of Cloud Computing

In spite of its many benefits, as mentioned above, Cloud Computing also has its disadvantages. Businesses, especially smaller ones, need to be aware of these cons before going in for this technology.

- **Internet access:** usually no Internet access means no Cloud access.
- **Security:** Cloud data centers can be high security and highly managed, but also low security and badly managed. How can you check if this is the case?
- **Privacy:** in case of public or hybrid offerings it may be uncertain where your data is stored in combination with varying national and international legislation on privacy, you never know who can access your data.
- **Service level agreement:** does your agreement allow for flexibility and scalability?
- **Vendor lock-in:** staying with a provider that doesn't meet your needs, just to avoid the troublesome and risky process of migrating your cloud services.

Exam preparation: chapter 1

'Get it' questions

1. Describe the four types of Cloud Deployment Models and give an example of each of the four types.
2. What are the differences between SaaS, PaaS and IaaS?
3. Name the key factors that have contributed to the present day existence of "the Cloud".
4. Which two other developments were needed to make the Internet accessible to everyone?
5. Take a look at the Wikipedia website and search for "virtualization". Which different types of virtualization are mentioned here? Compare these types with Kuznetzky's types.
6. Explain why the storage of health care data is an example of single purpose architecture.
7. What does SOA mean?
8. Name four drivers and four limitations of Cloud Computing.

Exam Terms

Cloud Computing, Cloud characteristics, deployment models (Private, Public, Community and Hybrid), service models (SaaS, PaaS and IaaS), evolution of Cloud Computing, LAN, Internet, virtualization, managed services, Cloud Computing architectures: multipurpose, multi-tenancy, Service Oriented Architecture (SOA), drivers and limitations of Cloud Computing.

Implementing and Managing Cloud Computing: exam specifications

After reading chapter 2, you understand the principles of Implementing and Managing Cloud Computing (20%)

2.1 You understand the building of Local Cloud environment (10%)

You can:

2.1.1   Describe the main components of a local Cloud environment and how they are interconnected

2.1.2   Describe the use of secured access to a Local Area Network

2.1.3   Describe the risks of connecting a local Cloud network to the public Internet

2.2 You understand the principles of managing Cloud services (10%)

You can:

2.2.1   Describe the use of IT Service Management principles (ISO/IEC 20000) in a Cloud environment

2.2.2   Explain the management of service levels in a Cloud environment

2. Implementing and Managing Cloud Computing

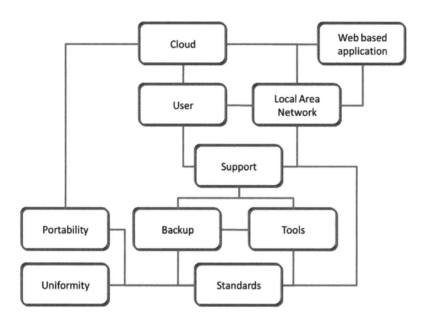

2.1 Building a local Cloud environment

It can be said that a local Cloud environment is not much different from the traditional data center. However, by employing modern Cloud technology and architectures large organizations can benefit from the better of two worlds, both the private data center and the Cloud. A private data center provides you with complete control and your own internal security mechanisms rule. In addition, a Private Cloud gives you flexibility, enhanced scalability and enhanced accessibility for employees; for example supporting secure home working places using VPN and MPLS connections. Nowadays only large companies have their own data center.

2.1.1 Main components of a local Cloud environment

This paragraph gives a quick overview of the main hardware and software components of a local Cloud environment as well as some key performance criteria.

Main hardware components

- Blade server arrays server chassis housing multiple thin, modular electronic circuit boards, known as server blades. Each blade is a server in its own right, often dedicated to a single application, such as web hosting, virtualization, and cluster computing.
- Local Area Network (LAN)
- Storage
    - o Storage Area Network (SAN): dedicated network that provides access to consolidated, data storage
    - o Network Attached Storage (NAS)
- Load balancer: provides the means by which instances of applications can be provisioned and de-provisioned automatically, without requiring changes to the network or its configuration. It automatically handles the increases and decreases in capacity and adapts its distribution decisions based on the capacity available at the time a request is made.

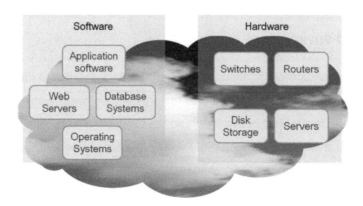

Main software components

- Virtualization software (e.g., VMware)
- Cloud application software (e.g., CRM, Office suite, ERP, etc.)
- Database software (e.g., Oracle, IBM DB2, Microsoft SQL, etc.)
- Middleware: software that connects software components or enterprise applications and is the software layer that lies between the operating system and the applications on each side of a distributed computer network
- Operating systems (Microsoft, UNIX, OpenStack)

Architectural considerations:

In order to make maximum use of the interoperability principle of Cloud Computing it is important to standardize the architecture by using standard protocols and other building blocks that are location and vendor independent. Some examples of these are: virtualization, SAN and Blade servers, load balancing. To manage the infrastructure a central management console is needed. OpenStack is an example of a cloud operating system orchestrating all these elements.

Furthermore, we need to consider the security and service continuity of a local Cloud environment. Ideally it consists of multiple sites to assist with disaster prevention and recovery (business continuity), uses proper backup mechanisms and data storage replication across sites, and uses common and high security elements like firewalls, DMZ, security software, role based user profiles, etc.

Successful Cloud solutions require specific performance criteria. Some examples are:
- Physical components: Scalability of server and storage capacity
- Storage: SAN performance (read, write and delete times)
- Internal processes: Connection speed, Deployment latency and Lag time

2.1.2 Secured access

In order to grant secure and efficient access to the local Cloud environment from remote locations a Virtual Private Network (VPN) is needed, potentially combined with Multiprotocol Label Switching (MPLS). A VPN combined with MPLS is typically made up from a central computing environment, remote office locations and other remote employee locations like their home office.

Key benefits of a VPN and MPLS for building a Hybrid Cloud

A Cloud VPN and MPLS connection can help you to create a secure and fast connection between your Private Cloud and your remote users, external service providers and Public or Community Cloud providers. In order to achieve high security you create your own virtual Private Cloud within the public environment and connect it to your private environment.

The key benefits are:
- Remote secure connectivity; extends your LAN/WAN to a global scale.
- Cheaper than using traditional rented network connections; it makes use of standard Internet connections through DSL, fiber or cable connections or fast mobile data connections.
- More mobility for employees; improve productivity for employees working from their home.

Architectural considerations

For most VPN connections the principle of IP tunneling is employed. You create a secure point-to-point connection, a tunnel, through which you transfer your data. Technically tunneling is the process of placing a packet within another packet and sending it over a network. Three different protocols are needed for tunneling: carrier protocol - used by the network, encapsulating protocol - 'wrapping' the original data and passenger protocol - original data; i.e., IP.

Key building blocks are: IP tunneling, Security (Firewalls, Internet Protocol Security Protocol (IPsec), Encryption, and Authentication, Authorization and Accounting servers (AAA)).

Multiprotocol Label Switching (MPLS) is a mechanism in high-performance telecommunications networks that directs data from one network node to the next based on short path labels rather than long network addresses, avoiding complex lookups in a routing table. The labels identify virtual links (paths) between distant nodes rather than endpoints. MPLS can encapsulate packets of various network protocols. MPLS supports a range of access technologies. (*Source Wikipedia, as viewed on 18-09-2015)*

2.1.3 Risks of connecting a local Cloud network to the public Internet

The IT Security Network Company SecPoint asks an interesting question concerning Cloud Internet security:

> *"Are companies really willing to risk having all their information, data, privacy, and software handled in a virtual Cloud—a place where they're most susceptible to hack attacks and cyber invasions?"*
>
> *(www.secpoint.com)*

Storing data in the Cloud looks a lot like storing your precious goods in a bank vault, but in the case of the bank you know where they are, and in which locker your goods are stored. In the case of the Cloud, how well are your data protected against theft?

Key considerations will have to do with security of data. With Internet based Cloud services data can be stored in any place in the world without you knowing it. Also, what happens to your data when you are not using it? Is it automatically put under lock and key, or are your databases still open to the outside world? A lot of responsibility lies with the provider.

Secpoint formulates this as follows:

"Cloud providers have a responsibility in ensuring that there are no exploitable bugs in their SaaS collection by deploying penetration testing and vulnerability assessment procedures on each and every last program they have available. Packaged or outsourced application code must be sorted out, examined, and monitored from the inside out as well."

There also lies a heavy responsibility with the customers. They need to check if their provider has everything under control. The customer for example will need to look how data Protection and partitioning is organized in the Cloud environment. Several measures need to be taken to keep data safe. Some of the available options are having a wall between data from different clients, zoning, hidden storage and role based customer and user profiles (this means anonymity, you do not know who your neighbors are).

2.2 The principles of managing Cloud services

2.2.1 IT Service Management principles in a Cloud environment

Outsourcing IT services to a Cloud provider does not mean that a customer (large corporation or SME/SMB) can sit back and leave everything to the provider. Even if infrastructure management, operational IT and management of services are outsourced, the customer still needs to focus on business-IT alignment and IT governance. In order to check the provider's performance and compliance a proper IT Service Management needs to be set up, and preferably in an auditable way. Proven frameworks; i.e., the Information Technology Infrastructure Library® (ITIL), Business Information Management and Application Management and IT Service Management standards; i.e., ISO/IEC 20000-1:2011, ISO/IEC TR 20000-9:2015, can be used, both by the provider and the customer.

Cloud Service Provider

Cloud service providers are no different to traditional IT service providers in relation to their need to provide quality, cost-effective, secure and available IT services. The Service Provider needs to be in control of the complete supply chain consisting of data center operations, network and Internet providers and other providers like SaaS solution partners.

A well proven standard for IT Service Management with both internal and external audit mechanisms is ISO/IEC 20000-1:2011. In this standard there are four process areas: IT and the

Business, Designing for service, Control of IT services and Support of IT services. The scope covers both Management and Improvement of ITSM. Additionally ISO/IEC TR 20000-9:2015 can now be used, which provides guidance on the use of ISO/IEC 20000-1:2011 for service providers delivering cloud services. It is applicable to different categories of cloud service, such as those defined in ISO/IEC 17788/ITU-T Y.3500 and ISO/IEC 17789/ITU-T Y.3502.

Cloud customer

Customers of Cloud Computing and cloud based services should expect, and demand, at least the same levels of service as that is provided by traditional IT service providers and internal IT organizations. A corporate or public sector customer of Cloud services needs to make sure that proper governance mechanisms are in place. Main elements are a good Service level management (SLM) process on the side of the provider, and proper audit standards and instruments. A provider is preferably ISO certified to ensure that a good internal audit system is in place covering the complete supply and demand chain. Further business focused standards may also be of benefit for the customer's own IT Service Management organization.

Examples of these are:

- COBIT™ 5 – Framework for the governance and management of enterprise IT
- ISO/IEC 38500:2015; Information technology -- Governance of IT for the organization
- ISO/IEC 15504-1:2004; Information technology -- Process assessment (also known as SPICE)

Questions to ask the Cloud provider:

- How are audits performed?
- Where are the servers located, and which legislation applies to the data?
- What continuity plans are in place for recovering data, infrastructure and applications?
- What are the provisions when a service changes or ends (service life cycle and end of life)?
- What are the provisions if we want to migrate to another provider (contract life cycle and end of life)?

Service level management (SLA)

We need to realize that there are different Service level requirements (SLRs) for the different Cloud deployment models. For public clouds they need to be highly standardized and available to everybody and should not be used for critical data. Examples are e-mail, productivity applications and storage. For Private Clouds, the SLA needs to cover all IT services & systems and the network. Service levels depend on the provider. And finally, for Hybrid Clouds, it will be a mix of the above because they are in fact any combination of Public and Private Clouds. Therefore service levels may vary.

2.2.2 Management of service levels in a Cloud environment

As a customer you will want the provider to comply with several quality specifications, and the corresponding processes to be in place.

The ISO/IEC 20000-1:2011 standard comprises several processes which are important for a Cloud data center or provider. As a customer you will want to see proven strategies and implementation of the most essential service management processes to guarantee compliance with these quality criteria. The following table shows the ISO/IEC 20000-1:2011 quality specifications for information systems and how they are managed.

Component	Consisting of	Purpose	Quality specifications
Information System	− People − Processes − Technology − Partners	To manage information	− Availability − Capacity − Performance − Security
Support	− Changes, system restoration in case of failure − Maintenance	To ensure performance according to the agreed requirements	− Scalability − Adjustability − Portability − Interoperability − Confidentiality

ISO/IEC 20000-1:2011 specification: processes

The goal of an ISO/IEC 20000 certification and/or follow-up audit is to check if the organization fulfills the ISO/IEC 20000 requirements. A number of requirements are mandatory. One of these is the documentation of the ISO/IEC 20000 processes. However, this is not enough.
The organization; i.e., your Cloud provider also needs to demonstrate that members of staff are familiar with these processes and adhere to the procedures and working instructions.

ISO/IEC TR 20000-9:2015

ISO/IEC TR 20000-9:2015 provides guidance on the use of ISO/IEC 20000-1:2011 for service providers delivering cloud services. The applicability of ISO/IEC 20000-1 is independent of the type of technology or service model used to deliver the services. All requirements in ISO/IEC 20000-1 can be applicable to cloud service providers.

The structure of ISO/IEC TR 20000-9:2015 does not follow the structure of ISO/IEC 20000-1. The guidance is presented as a set of scenarios that can address many of the typical activities of a cloud service provider. The guidance in ISO/IEC TR 20000-9:2015 can also be useful for customers of cloud service providers.

This part of ISO/IEC TR 20000-9:2015 can be used as guidance for a cloud service provider in designing, managing, or improving an SMS to support cloud services.

ISO/IEC TR 20000-9:2015 does not add any requirements to those stated in ISO/IEC 20000-1 and does not state explicitly how evidence can be provided to an assessor or auditor. The scope of ISO/IEC TR 20000-9:2015 excludes any specifications for products or tools.

2.2.3 New emerging standard ISO/IEC 19086 for Management of service levels in a Cloud environment

Cloud service management shares some basic principles with traditional IT service management (ITSM). Cloud management tools help providers administrate the systems and applications that facilitate the on-demand service delivery model. The goal of these practices is to improve the efficiency of the cloud environment and achieve a high level of customer satisfaction.

Given the elastic, highly virtualized nature of cloud environments, there are some key differences in approaches to cloud service management and conventional IT service management. The two disciplines have different objectives, requiring tools that emphasize their individual requirements. Whereas the goals of traditional ITSM are effective SLA management, improved performance and streamlined billing, the goal of cloud service management is to orchestrate resources for fast provisioning, effective capacity management and ongoing service stability. Automation is vital to ensure efficiency and reduce costs.

The core elements of cloud service management mirror those of traditional ITSM -- including cloud service level agreement (SLA) management, cloud capacity management, availability management and billing -- and are applied to administrate a cloud delivery environment in a systemic way. In today's cloud service industry, the lack of standardization in SLAs and the use of SLAs as a potential marketing vehicle have resulted in a SLA jargon. On the other hand, the users are becoming more demanding in terms of service requirements, offered and guaranteed levels of quality, data protection, etc. Taking these facts into consideration, ISO/IEC JTC 1/SC 38 - Cloud Computing and Distributed Platforms is working on the new set of standards ISO/IEC 19086, which includes the following:

- ISO/IEC CD 19086-1; Information technology -- Cloud computing -- Service level agreement (SLA) framework and Technology -- Part 1: Overview and concepts
- ISO/IEC NP 19086-2; Information technology -- Cloud computing -- Service level agreement (SLA) framework and Technology -- Part 2: Metrics
- ISO/IEC NP 19086-3; Information technology -- Cloud computing -- Service level agreement (SLA) framework and Technology -- Part 3: Core requirements

Exam preparation: chapter 2

'Get it' questions

1. Draw a local Cloud environment with its main components and how they are interconnected.
2. Name the key benefits of using a VPN combined with MPLS.
3. There are risks of connecting a local Cloud network to the public Internet. One of the risks is that there lies a heavy responsibility with the customers. They need to check if their provider has everything under control. The customer for example will need to look how data Protection and partitioning is organized in the Cloud environment. Several measures need to be taken to keep data safe. What are the available options?
4. The goal of an ISO/IEC 20000 certification and/or follow-up audit is to check if the organization fulfills the ISO/IEC 20000 requirements. A number of requirements are mandatory. One of these is the documentation of the ISO/IEC 20000 processes. Name three process groups including the processes per group.

Exam Terms

Implementing and managing Cloud computing, local Cloud environment, software, hardware, VPN, MPLS, risks, service management, Cloud provider and SLA.

Using the Cloud: exam specifications

After reading chapter 3, you understand the principles of Using the Cloud (15%)

3.1 You know how users can access the Cloud (5%)

You can:

3.1.1   Describe how to access Web Applications through a Web Browser

3.1.2   Describe the Cloud Web Access Architecture

3.1.3   Describe the use of a Thin Client

3.1.4   Describe the use of mobile devices in accessing the Cloud

3.2 You understand how Cloud Computing can be used for business processes (5%)

You can:

3.2.1   Identify the impact of Cloud Computing on the primary processes of an organization

3.2.2   Describe the role of standard applications in collaboration

3.3 You understand how Service Providers can use the Cloud (5%)

You can:

3.3.1   Explain how using Cloud Computing changes the relation between vendors and customers

3.3.2   Identify benefits and risks of providing Cloud based services

3. Using the Cloud

3.1 Accessing the Cloud

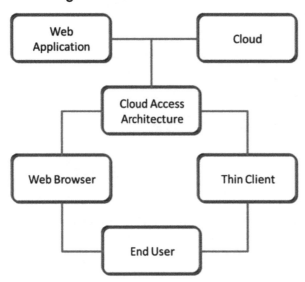

3.1.1 How to access Web Applications through a Web Browser

Getting connected to "the Cloud" to access Cloud based SaaS solutions like Office solutions seems to be very simple indeed. All you need is a PC or laptop, choose an Internet browser, get an Internet connection and a solution by a Cloud service provider. For example, as a private user you buy a laptop, connect it to the wireless router provided to you by your Internet Service Provider (ISP), choose a browser of your liking, e.g., Google Chrome, Microsoft IE or Mozilla Firefox, and get onto the Internet. Say you decided you want a free web based office solution, find a provider, subscribe for free (but limited) account, and you are in business.

However, for businesses, small or big, it takes 'two to Tango'. In this case you will first have to determine why you want to start using Cloud solutions (price, flexibility, scalability/elasticity, access any time, any place from any device,…), then what you want to use (Office solution, File storage and sharing, online collaboration, professional applications like CRM, or a virtual desktop for your sales staff,…) and finally how you want to access these services with what basic infrastructure.

Do you have your own server farm and LAN, or are you a small SMB/SME and want to get rid of all that equipment in your small office? And what about privacy and security?

Accessing the Cloud is still a straightforward and simple concept. You need access to the Internet! Or maybe you call this, in case of your Private Cloud plans, the intranet. To help us understand how and why we need the Internet it is good to have a quick look at a few basic concepts. The first one is the Internet. Let us start with a definition 'from the Cloud' (Wikipedia).

According to a Cloud based source (Wikipedia):

> The Internet is a global system of interconnected computer networks that use the standard Internet protocol suite (TCP/IP) to link several billion devices worldwide. It is a network of networks that consists of millions of private, public, academic, business, and government networks of local to global scope, linked by a broad array of electronic, wireless, and optical networking technologies. The Internet carries an extensive range of information resources and services, such as the inter-linked hypertext documents and applications of the World Wide Web (WWW), the infrastructure to support email, and peer-to-peer networks for file sharing and telephony.
>
> http://en.wikipedia.org/wiki/Internet / as viewed on 16-06-2015

One of the key architectural components of the Internet is the standard Internet protocol suite (TCP/IP). Every device wanting to access the Internet requires an address to be identified and recognized; this is called the IP address. Furthermore we need to realize that it is a global system of interconnected computer networks meaning that you will be connected to the rest of the world.

Finally, these networks are "linked by a broad array of electronic, wireless and optical networking technologies." In order to get these concepts into perspective we need to look at the Open Systems Interconnection model (OSI model), the TCP/IP model and a definition of Internet.

Open Systems Interconnection model (OSI model)

The model is a product of the Open Systems Interconnection project at the International Organization for Standardization (ISO), maintained by the identification ISO/IEC 7498-1. It was published in 1984 by both the ISO, as standard ISO 7498, and the renamed CCITT (now called the Telecommunications Standardization Sector of the International Telecommunication Union or ITU-T) as standard X.200. The OSI model was developed to help standardize the functions of communications systems in terms of layers. Cloud Computing, because of its characteristics of sharing resources and interconnectivity needs a high degree of standardization of its components, both on the provider and customer side. We can map standards to each layer of the OSI model to see what is needed in the chain between transmitting and receiving data.

TRANSMIT		RECEIVE
7. Application layer		7. Application layer
6. Presentation layer		6. Presentation layer
5. Session layer		5. Session layer
4. Transport layer		4. Transport layer
3. Network layer		3. Network layer
2. Data link layer		2. Data link layer
1. Physical layer		1. Physical layer
Physical Link		

A simple representation of the OSI-model

Now let us map some of the standard protocols onto this model. Starting on the physical layer, you will need some kind of physical or wireless connection to the Internet. This can be done in many ways: wired through your LAN connection, for this you need a network interface card (NIC), for which there are many so-called IEEE standards, and an Ethernet cable (RJ45-cat. 4 or 5). Now you have established an Ethernet connection (layer 2). Next you need a transport medium, the Transmission Control Protocol (TCP), and an Internet Protocol (IP) address (layers 3/4). We have now covered the hardware side of things. The same can also be achieved with a wireless connection in the office, by using public hotspots or by connecting a smart device to the Internet through a cellphone network or even with a satellite link.

Next we need to establish a session with an application, the session layer (NetBIOS, sockets) takes care of opening, closing and managing applications (layer 5). In the next layer we take care of presenting the data (ASCII) (layer 6). Finally we can use our web-based or Cloud applications through layer 6: access a www website (http), make secure payments with a safe connection (https), receive E-mail through the post office protocol (POP), send mail with the Simple Mail Transfer Protocol (SMTP) or transfer files with the file transfer protocol (FTP).

Summarizing we can state that from a business perspective we need to establish our business requirements concerning speed and capacity (do we need a simple cable connection or a secure rented line, copper cable or dark fiber, MPLS), mobility and mobile security (wireless through unsecure hotspots = free or personal connections through our cellphone data connection), security (VPN and encryption).
In the next paragraph we will have a closer look at the architectural building blocks needed to access the Cloud.

3.1.2 Cloud Web Access Architecture

One of the key architectural features of Cloud Computing is the use of standard protocol and other design standards. The following table relates the OSI-model layers we discussed in the previous paragraph to some of these standards and for what they are used in the chain between transmission of data over the Internet to receiving them on your Internet enabled device (PC, thin client, smart phone, tablet, etc.)

Protocol/standard (examples)	ISO/OSI model layer	Description
HTTP	Application	Hypertext Transfer Protocol (HTTP); foundation for the world wide web (WWW)

VT
 	
RTSE
	Presentation	On the SASE sub layer (specific application service element)
		   – Virtual terminal
		On the CASE Sub layer (common application service element)
		   – Reliable Transfer Service Element

API-sockets Sockets	Session	Application programming interface (API); allows application programs to control and use network sockets
TCP SSL	Transport	Transmission Control Protocol Secure Sockets Layer; a protocol for encrypting information over the Internet.
IP	Internet/Network	Transmission Control Protocol/Internet Protocol
Ethernet, IEEE 802.3	Data Link/Link	Carrier Sense Multiple Access / Collision Detection (CSMA/CD) Defining the physical layer and data link layer's media access control (MAC) of wired Ethernet. (Wi-Fi equivalent: 802.11a,b/g,n)
10BASE-T	Physical	Fixed line (cable, LAN, WAN) or wireless connection

Another key component of Cloud Computing architecture is virtualization. One or more layers of the OSI model can be virtualized. We will not go into this in any detail here. If you are interested in this topic you will be able to find several articles on the Internet. An example of an online article concerning layers 1-3 can be found on http://prsync.com/oracle/networks-and-virtualization-413234/

3.1.3 Using a Thin Client

In the past we were used to accessing central computer facilities and functions from a simple device called a terminal. However, this was not very close to getting connected to the whole world like via the Internet. The connection was point-to-point between the terminal and the mainframe. As early as the 1960's a form of virtualization was used to divide the powerful mainframe processor or processors into several separate machines, each performing their own task. The next step was ever more powerful personal computers and client server systems. In this scenario there was still part of the actual application on the local device, the so-called client application. With the emergence of Cloud Computing most of the necessary computing power now runs on the systems in the Cloud; a bit like the mainframe days we can say. So the last step is to replace the expensive PCs from our offices and replace them by a kind of modern terminal. This is gaining popularity among businesses and enterprises of all sizes: combining graphically powerful thin client terminals with Cloud Computing resources.

Traditionally, a thin client is a bare bones computer that allows users to access programs, files, and functionality that is hosted on another computer, typically a physical server located somewhere else in the office. The server pushes the operating system, programs and information to the thin client when a user logs on. The thin client is little more than a computer terminal that acts as a vessel through which information and functionality are provided.

For businesses seeking enhanced security, higher user satisfaction, cost savings and improved accessibility for remote users, combining thin clients with Cloud Computing offers an effective solution. To summarize the benefits:

- **Greater security and enhanced resource management:** Thin clients offer network administrators peace of mind by eliminating the chance for physical data loss and lessening concerns about client integrity.
- **End user satisfaction:** Bringing a thin client into a Cloud Computing environment gives end users all of the benefits of a desktop PC without the headaches and challenges that typically accompany "fat" computers.
- **Cost effective and "green":** Because thin clients have few (if any) moving parts, there are few physical items that can break, which means a longer life span for every terminal. And because these machines let the cloud do much of the heavy lifting when it comes to making computations, saving documents and sharing files, their power consumption is much lower, leading to lower costs and reduced energy needs.

- **Greater remote accessibility:** Cloud Computing and thin clients allow for much greater flexibility in remote access than more traditional computing environments. Users can access their files, programs and email no matter where they are, increasing productivity without increasing information technology challenges.

3.1.4 Using mobile devices in accessing the Cloud

Can we still imagine a world without a smartphone? Since the emergence of mass cellphone usage the 'phone' seems to have come of age. Cellphone services using servers first appeared when we started to send short text messages (SMS), and this was quickly followed by other solutions like the transmission of pictures (MMS). Receiving email on a smartphone is now a standard function, e.g., SMTP and Exchange. The present day hardware platforms and operating systems for smartphones have transformed them into web-enabled personal devices.
Next came the 3G enabled tablets, and next... The future will tell.

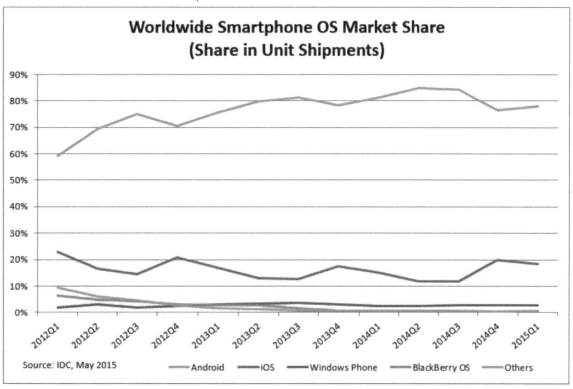

The present day leading smartphone operating systems are:

- Google Android
- Apple iOS
- Windows Phone
- Blackberry

Although there is a high degree of interoperability between the different cellphone networks and providers (maybe with the exception of Blackberry), smartphone apps and services can generally not be used on another operating system. To increase their market share software providers often develop apps for the other leading platforms. Developing these for 'the Cloud' would mean universal accessibility. An example is Exchange mail in combination with the push email function on a smartphone; the user can update his/her agenda, contact list, notes and task list on the road, and receive and send email. All of these instances are automatically updated on the Exchange server. When the user logs on to his/her Exchange account in the office everything is already synchronized.

Some downsides for business users can be found with the present day technologies. There may be security and privacy issues like having your business data on removable media like SD cards, and doing business on-the-road may be compromised by shoulder surfing; i.e., people looking over your shoulder at your screen in a waiting room.

The problem may be tackled by a user awareness campaign. Also, a business manager should consider the way smart devices are used by their staff. Most of them will have one of these devices themselves and used to being constantly online and connected to services like iTunes, Facebook and streaming media. For example, most iPhone and Android users have so many apps installed that this may distract them from work. In this respect, online time and data usage could also become a very high cost for your organization.

3.2 How Cloud Computing can support business processes

3.2.1 Identify the impact of Cloud Computing on the primary processes of an organization

First we need to determine what (type of) Cloud service model we need to support our business. Depending on this choice we can also determine how we integrate our own, present or future, infrastructure with the Internet and our Cloud provider's infrastructure. If we only need a virtual desktop for our sales staff that is on the road, we can go for the Infrastructure as a Service model (IaaS).

Typical IaaS services cover the first four layers of the OSI model. Or maybe we need many different kinds of software development platforms with the elasticity between low capacity during the design and programming stages, and high capacity during the testing stages we can opt for the Platform as a Service (PaaS) model. Since we are in fact programming our own Application Programming Interfaces (API), we only need OSI coverage up to layer five, and maybe part of layer 6.

However, for most customers of the Cloud the Software as a Service (SaaS) model is the most applicable. In the SaaS model the customers' needs to take care of their own Internet (or intranet/ local network) capable device to connect. Given all the connection options that are available to us these days, this actually means any time, any place and from any device. However, this will depend on your requirements for mobility versus security and privacy, how much you can afford in terms of money, and also other requirements like speed, capacity and elasticity.

At the present day there are already many typical business solutions available from the Cloud. The following table gives you an overview of SaaS business solution examples with possible target audiences.

Category	Target audience	Examples
Customer Relationship Management (CRM)	Large corporations, public sector organizations or NGO's	Salesforce.com, SugarCRM, NetSuite
Enterprise Resource Planning (ERP)	Large corporations, public sector organizations or NGO's	NetSuite, Compiere (open source), Microsoft Dynamics AX ERP
HR solutions	Large corporations, public sector organizations or NGO's Small enterprises	Taleo, FinancialForce.com Human Capital Management (HCM) Natural HR
IT Service Management	Large corporations, public sector organizations or NGO's	ServiceNow
Finance & accounting	Large corporations, public sector organizations or NGO's	Intacct, NetSuite
Web design and management	Large and small enterprises and all other type of organization	Joomla (free), Adobe Creative Cloud, XSitePro
E-mail (professional)	Large enterprises and SME's/SMB's	Microsoft Exchange online, Gmail (Google Apps for business), Cisco WebEx Mail, IBM LotusLive iNotes
Webmail	Small SME's/SMB's	Gmail, Outlook.com, etc…
Office suites	Large and small enterprises	Microsoft Office 365, Google Apps for Work, Zoho Office Suite
E-Business	Medium to large Enterprises Small enterprises	Capgemini Immediate, Oracle RIO Gogiro, Google OpenEntry.com
Online Storage	SME's/SMB's	Google Drive, DropBox, Microsoft OneDrive, Amazon S3
Collaboration	Large enterprises and organizations SME's/SMB's	Microsoft SharePoint Online, CloudShare DropBox
Video conferencing	SME's/SMB's	Skype, WebEx Meeting Center

Having these solutions from the Cloud will give you additional benefits to running these on your own data center. You can in fact combine solutions from your own private (Cloud) environment with public solutions creating your own tailor made Hybrid Cloud. For example in purchasing and manufacturing Cloud can enable collaboration with suppliers, and by using exchange and sharing platforms for sales, advertising and marketing you can promote and enable interaction with potential customers and the market through social media like Facebook. Many starting, but also established artists in the musical industry now use this mechanism as their primary sales channel. Another example could be facilitation of an easy way to register customer contacts in the CRM system by sales people on the road.

3.2.2 The role of standard applications in collaboration

Social media like Facebook, LinkedIn and Twitter have led the way to modern forms of collaboration. Sharing and working together on documents is now easy because of services like Google Drive and Dropbox. Video conferencing and free Internet calls are possible because of Skype, and we can go on from here. New free Cloud services emerge in rapid succession, and the more successful of these are further developed into professional Cloud services. For example Google's Gmail has now a business equivalent, and combined with the other Google Apps for business Google is now becoming a serious Cloud SaaS provider.

3.3 How Service Providers can use the Cloud

3.3.1 How Cloud Computing changes the relation between vendors and customers

With ever more IT services being moved to the Cloud IT providers will have to rethink their service models in the Cloud way. What is certain to happen is another relationship with their customers. Because providers take over a large part of the customer's IT systems and service management they need to be ready to rewrite their SLAs to demonstrate to their customers that they can and will deliver most of the value chain. Some other aspects to consider are customer privacy (you are now virtually running your customer's business processes), and the need for a proper and transparent audit trail (large and corporate customers will demand proof of compliance to standards like ISO/IEC 20000 and COBIT®).

3.3.2 Benefits and risks of providing Cloud based services

With the development of the Cloud business model new business opportunities, but also challenges arise for IT Service providers. Traditional data center providers are quickly rebuilding their traditional infrastructure services into IaaS, PaaS and SaaS services. Existing resources have a new lease of life because of the multi-tenancy principle. More users on one platform add the economies of scale to the equation. Software developers are now developing on PaaS platforms and are able to decrease the time in which their applications can be designed, built and tested.

An even greater benefit may be the fact that the new flexible solutions from the Cloud can support the rapidly changing enterprise workplace. With their long experience in Service Management and IT, Service Management leading hosting service providers can become an important factor in the Cloud market. Uniquely positioned to capitalize on the managed services market; not every business is ready for a self-service model.

Of course there are a number of challenges that need to be faced. Not every provider is ready to deal with standards, complex security issues arising from the Cloud, high performance demands in combination with flexibility (elasticity), data compliance legislation and availability and continuity issues; the Cloud is open 24/7!

Exam preparation: chapter 3

'Get it' questions

1. List the 'basic ingredients' needed to access Web Applications through a Web Browser.
2. Describe the key architectural features of Cloud Computing.
3. What is a Thin Client and why should we use a Thin Client?
4. At the present day there are already many typical business solutions available from the Cloud. The following table gives you an overview of SaaS business solution examples with possible target audiences. Fill in the missing text.

Category	Target audience	Examples
	Large corporations, public sector organizations or NGO's	Salesforce.com, SugarCRM, NetSuite
Enterprise Resource Planning (ERP)	Large corporations, public sector organizations or NGO's	
HR solutions		Taleo, FinancialForce.com Human Capital Management (HCM) Natural HR
	Large corporations, public sector organizations or NGO's	ServiceNow
Finance & accounting	Large corporations, public sector organizations or NGO's	
	Large and small enterprises	Microsoft Office 365, Google Apps for Work, Zoho Office Suite
Video conferencing	SME's/SMB's	

5. Using Cloud Computing changes the relation between vendors and customers. What aspects change?
6. Describe two benefits and two risks of providing Cloud based services.

Exam Terms

Accessing the Cloud, OSI model, Cloud Web Access Architecture, thin client, mobile devices, Cloud Computing in the business and service providers.

Security and compliance: exam specifications

After reading chapter 4, you understand the principles of Security and compliance (20%).

4.1 You understand the security risks of Cloud Computing and you know mitigating measures (10%)

You can:

4.1.1   Describe the security risks in the Cloud

4.1.2   Describe measures mitigating security risks

4.2 You understand managing identity and privacy in the Cloud (10%)

You can:

4.2.1   Describe the main aspects of Identity management

4.2.2   Describe privacy and compliance issues and safeguards in Cloud Computing

4. Security and compliance

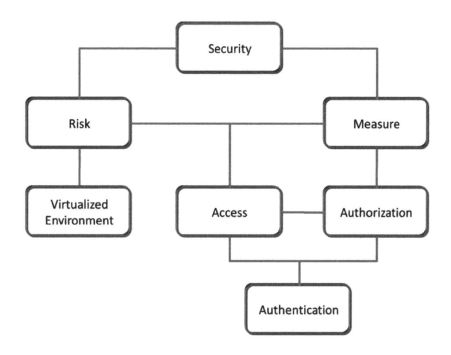

Cloud Computing means sharing, the Internet, multi-tenancy, a mix of free and non-free services, data stored in any place of the world, anonymous customer, unclear SLAs, many standards are used on the technical side. However, hardly any, like ISO/IEC 20000, are used for compliance.

By realizing the security risks, a customer will be able to assess prospective providers and choose the right services that will not compromise their own compliance to legislation and regulations.

4.1 Security risks of Cloud Computing and mitigating measures

Since Cloud Computing contains many new architectural and design features we first need to look at the different types of security risks. A group of leading IT providers like HP, Oracle, Qualys, Microsoft and Rackspace as well as customers like Bank of America have joined forces in the Cloud Security Alliance (CSA).

The Cloud Security Alliance (CSA) is a not-for-profit organization with a mission to promote the use of best practices for providing security assurance within Cloud Computing, and to provide education on the uses of Cloud Computing to help secure all other forms of computing. (Source: Cloudsecurityalliance.org).

In 2013 it published a white paper discussing Cloud security issues. The paper is named "Cloud Security Alliance The Notorious Nine: Cloud Computing Top Threats in 2013" and can be found at: https://cloudsecurityalliance.org/group/top-threats/

4.1.1 Security risks in the Cloud

The top threats to Cloud Computing according to the CSA are, in no specific order: Data Breaches, Data Loss, Account or Service Traffic Hijacking, Insecure Interfaces and API, Denial-of-Service, Malicious Insiders, Abuse of Cloud Services, Insufficient Due Diligence and Shared Technology Vulnerabilities. *(Source: 'Cloud Security Alliance The Notorious Nine: Cloud Computing Top Threats in 2013.")* Let us have a closer look at these risks.

Data Breaches
Data in the Cloud has many advantages, but can be compromised in many ways. It can be altered or deleted without a backup; it may be unlinked from its context or accessed by unauthorized people.

Data Loss
Data in the Cloud has many advantages, but can be compromised in many ways. It can be altered or deleted without a backup; it may be unlinked from its context or accessed by unauthorized people.

Account or Service Traffic Hijacking
Most private users of E-mail and the Internet will be aware of fraudulent tactics like phishing, password hacking and identity theft. Passwords giving access to Cloud services go outside your own company IT domain, and therefore can be compromised. For businesses this can mean they are vulnerable to industrial espionage or can lose important business data or processes.

Insecure Interfaces and API
Application interfaces, or APIs, are key components for most Cloud services. If these interfaces are not properly designed for security they can become a risk 'waiting to happen'.

Denial-of-service

Denial-of-service attacks are attacks meant to prevent users of a cloud service from being able to access their data or their applications. By forcing the victim cloud service to consume inordinate amounts of finite system resources such as processor power, memory, disk space or network bandwidth, the attacker (or attackers, as is the case in Distributed Denial-of-service (DDoS) attacks) causes an intolerable system slowdown and leaves all of the legitimate service users confused and angry as to why the service isn't responding.

Malicious Insiders

If Cloud providers are a cross-section of our society, statistically seen, some of their staff or sub-contractor staff may be untrustworthy.

Abuse of Cloud Services

Many Cloud providers give very easy, and sometimes free for a trial period, access to their services. Registration is relatively anonymous and can and will attract 'darker customers' like spammers and hackers. Your Cloud provider may not only host your data and applications, but also malicious software.

Insufficient Due Diligence

Moving into the Cloud may make it more difficult for organizations to prove their compliance to legislation and regulations during external audits, e.g., EDP or IT-audit.

Shared Technology Vulnerabilities

A multi-tenant architecture has its own challenges. Some components may not have been developed for this type of use and may cause security issues.

4.1.2 Measures mitigating security risks

An objective way to ensure a provider's compliance with security best practices is to demand ISO certification. The standard ISO/IEC 20000:2011 contains a security paragraph, and an even more important certification is the ISO/IEC 27001:2013 standard; *Information technology -- Security techniques -- Information security management systems – Requirements,* and the way they have implemented the best practices described in ISO/IEC 27002:2013; *Information technology -- Security techniques -- Code of practice for information security management.*

The Cloud Security Association gives examples of what they call mitigating measures in their paper *"Top Threats to Cloud Computing" Version 1.0 – 2010.* We will give a brief summary of these measures in relation to the risks described by the Cloud Security Association, as well as some other possibilities. In the new version of the paper *"Cloud Security Alliance The Notorious Nine: Cloud Computing Top Threats in 2013"* a new section about controls has been added.

Data Breaches

Examples of mitigating measures that can be taken are authentication, audit, e.g., ISO/IEC 27001, Data Security, and authorization, as well as use of encryption and a proper backup strategy.

Controls

CCM DG-04: Data Governance - Retention Policy

CCM DG-05: Data Governance - Secure Disposal

CCM DG-06: Data Governance - Non-Production Data

CCM DG-07: Data Governance - Information Leakage

CCM DG-08: Data Governance - Risk Assessments

CCM IS-18: Information Security - Encryption

CCM IS-19: Information Security - Encryption Key Management

CCM SA-02: Security Architecture - User ID Credentials

CCM SA-03: Security Architecture - Data Security/Integrity

CCM SA-06: Security Architecture - Production/Non-Production Environments

CCM SA-07: Security Architecture - Remote User Multi-Factor Authentication

Data Loss

Examples of mitigating measures that can be taken are authentication, audit (i.e. ISO/IEC 27001, Data Security) and authorization, as well as use of encryption and a proper backup strategy.

Controls

CCM DG-04: Data Governance - Retention Policy

CCM DG-08: Data Governance - Risk Assessments

CCM RS-05: Resiliency - Environmental Risks

CCM RS-06: Resiliency - Equipment Location

Denial-of-Service

Controls

CCM IS-04: Information Security - Baseline Requirements

CCM OP-03: Operations Management - Capacity/Resource Planning

CCM RS-07: Resiliency - Equipment Power Failures

CCM SA-04: Security Architecture - Application Security

Shared technology vulnerabilities

Examples of mitigating measures that can be taken are enhanced operations procedures for monitoring and escalations when security breaches and application of good security practice for installation, configuration and application of patches.

Controls

CCM DG-03: Data Governance - Handling / Labeling / Security Policy

CCM IS-04: Information Security - Baseline Requirements

CCM IS-07: Information Security - User Access Policy

CCM IS-15: Information Security - Segregation of Duties

CCM IS-18: Information Security - Encryption

CCM IS-20: Information Security - Vulnerability / Patch Management

CCM SA-02: Security Architecture - User ID Credentials

CCM SA-09: Security Architecture - Segmentation

CCM SA-11: Security Architecture - Shared Networks

CCM SA-14: Security Architecture - Audit Logging / Intrusion Detection

Insecure interfaces and APIs

Examples of mitigating measures that can be taken are designing for security, proper testing methods, understanding how they interact with other interfaces and software, and strong authentication and access control.

Controls

CCM IS-08: Information Security - User Access Restriction/Authorization

CCM SA-03: Security Architecture - Data Security/Integrity

CCM SA-04: Security Architecture - Application Security

Insufficient Due Diligence

Examples of mitigating measures are assessing the financial health of the CSP or determining the length of time the cloud service provider has been in business

Controls

CCM DG-08: Data Governance - Risk Assessments

CCM IS-04: Information Security - Baseline Requirements

CCM IS-12: Information Security - Industry Knowledge / Benchmarking

CCM OP-03: Operations Management - Capacity / Resource Planning

CCM RI-01: Risk Management - Program

CCM RI-02: Risk Management - Assessments

CCM RS-01: Resiliency - Management Program

CCM RS-02: Resiliency - Impact Analysis

CCM RS -03: Resiliency - Business Continuity Planning

CCM SA-03: Security Architecture - Data Security / Integrity

CCM SA-04: Security Architecture - Application Security

CCM SA-08: Security Architecture - Network Security

CCM SA-09: Security Architecture - Segmentation

Malicious insiders

Examples of mitigating measures that can be taken are good HR vetting procedures, strong information security policies and procedures.

Controls

CCM CO-03: Compliance - Third Party Audits

CCM DG-01: Data Governance - Ownership / Stewardship

CCM DG-03: Data Governance - Handling / Labeling / Security Policy

CCM DG-07: Data Governance - Information Leakage

CCM FS-02: Facility Security - User Access

CCM FS-05: Facility Security - Unauthorized Persons Entry

CCM FS-06: Facility Security - Off-Site Authorization

CCM HR-01: Human Resources Security - Background Screening

CCM IS-06: Information Security - Policy Enforcement

CCM IS-08: Information Security - User Access Restriction / Authorization

CCM IS-10: Information Security - User Access Reviews

CCM IS-13: Information Security - Roles / Responsibilities

CCM IS-15: Information Security - Segregation of Duties

CCM IS-18: Information Security - Encryption

Abuse and nefarious use of Cloud Computing

Examples of mitigating measures that can be taken are validation of credentials, increased monitoring of traffic between customers and known suspicious sites.

Controls

CCM IS-24: Information Security - Incident Response Legal Preparation

CCM IS-26: Information Security - Acceptable Use

Unknown risk profile and account[1]

Examples of mitigating measures that can be taken are good SLA structures including Cloud provider compliance audits.

---

[1] From *"Top Threats to Cloud Computing" Version 1.0 – 2010, the controls were added in the 2013 version of the white paper.*

Account or service traffic hijacking

Examples of mitigating measures that can be taken are strong authentication techniques and monitoring of user behavior.

Controls

CCM IS-07: Information Security - User Access Policy

CCM IS-08: Information Security - User Access Restriction/Authorization

CCM IS-09: Information Security - User Access Revocation

CCM IS-10: Information Security - User Access Reviews

CCM IS-22: Information Security - Incident Management

CCM SA-02: Security Architecture - User ID Credentials

CCM SA-07: Security Architecture - Remote User Multi-Factor Authentication

CCM SA-14: Security Architecture - Audit Logging / Intrusion Detection

In the next paragraphs we will go into more detail in the areas of identity and privacy in the Cloud.

4.2 Managing identity and privacy in the Cloud

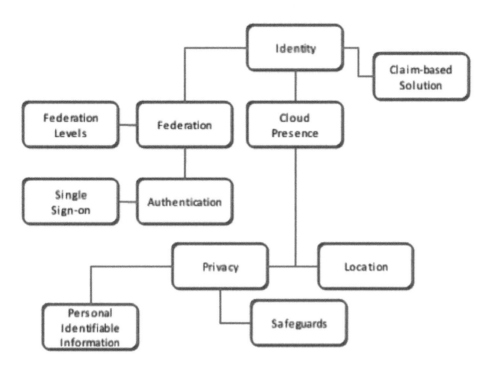

4.2.1 Main aspects of identity management

The effectiveness of the authentication process in normal, non-Cloud, situations depends on whether you are connected to a domain or not. If not, authentication will be local; your username and password are validated against account information stored on your own machine. The verification techniques will let you enter, even if your local account is not known. Only if the files you want to access are protected you will be asked for further credentials. Or, you are connected to a domain, active directory authentication is performed; you log on with your active directory (AD) account. In this case the Kerberos protocol is involved which can authenticate credentials without transmitting a password in either clear or scrambled form. Therefore it is impossible for the password to be cracked by a so-called password engine.

"Kerberos is a network authentication protocol. It is designed to provide strong authentication for client/server applications by using secret key cryptography." A free implementation of this protocol is available from the Massachusetts Institute of Technology.

source: http://web.mit.edu/kerberos/#what_is

Authentication in the Cloud

In a Private Cloud VM-ware can take over the role of the domain controller or security server, but in Hybrid Clouds' scenarios it becomes more diffused. In this case the additional security of VPN is needed for the connections between the Private and Public or Community Cloud parts.

The real problems appear with Public Clouds. In this scenario security can be handled or not handled in many ways, for example using the Lightweight Directory Access Protocol (LDAP), user-id and password lookup in a database or, if you are lucky, Kerberos. Furthermore, if you are using different solutions from the same or even different providers it is very unlikely that there is a single sign-on system in place like in your Private Cloud.

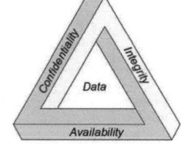

Since the Cloud is Internet based, security will have to be based on Internet-routable protocols, and such standardization between the different Cloud component infrastructure and service providers does not yet exist.

Triple-A: Authentication, Authorization and Accounting

Authentication, Authorization, and Accounting (AAA, pronounced "triple-A") is a technology that has been in use since before the days of the Internet as we know it today. These elements are the security corner stones of IP based network management and policy administration.

Authentication asks: "Who or what are you?" and refers to the process where someone's or something's identity is authenticated; examples are a digital certificate, a password and user-id or a security token.

Authorization asks: "What are you allowed to do?" and determines whether a particular entity is authorized for the requested action; access to certain data may be restricted, or there can be time restrictions preventing people from logging in to the system outside office hours.

Accounting wants to know, "What did you do?" and means the tracking of resource usage by users, and can for example be used as part of an audit trail, costing or billing, or capacity monitoring.

Identity management describes the management of individual principals, their authentication, authorization, and privileges within or across system and enterprise boundaries with the goal of increasing security and productivity while decreasing cost, downtime and repetitive tasks.

One way to think about Identity management is by imagining an enormous blueprint of an office building. It shows the rooms into which each person who works in the building can enter. The blueprint also shows what kind of key each person would need to open the door to get into that room, and what that person can do once they are there.

From: Aitoro, Jill R. (2008); The Basics: A Glossary of Federal Technology – Identity Management, www.nextgov.com

In her article, Jill Aitoro continues the metaphor and says *"A computer network is like the building, and each room represents a file, database or application on that network"* (Aitoro, 2008). Whether you work on the company network, intranet or are using Cloud solutions, organizations need proper identity control and access governance. There are several Identity management solutions available like Microsoft's Forefront and Azure Active Directory and IBM's Security Identity and Access Manager.

Typical characteristics of an Identity management system are:
- Role management; IT implementation of a business role
- Role hierarchy; a representation of an organization chart
- Separation of duties
- Group management; permissions are not given to people but to roles
- Self-service functions
- Password synchronization
- Digital Identity; presence and location determine available services and capabilities
- Federation Identity Management; enables single sign-on
- Etc.

Next we will discuss two examples of Identity management solutions, Single sign-on (SSO) and a special type of SSO called Federation Identity Management.

Single sign-on (SSO) for web services

One of the authentication challenges is formed by the fact that a Cloud based security infrastructure is distributed. Security features and algorithms are spread all over a certain domain. A solution for this problem is offered by the Single sign-on (SSO) principle. All distributed security elements are consolidated on one SSO server. As a result, a user only needs to sign on once using a security measure like a smart-card, a security token or an active directory (AD) account. SSO architecture uses the so-called SOAP protocol, a protocol for the exchange of information in the implementation of Web Services in the Cloud or any other network.

Federation Identity Management

Federation Identity Management, or the "federation" of identity, describes the technologies, standards and use-cases which serve to enable the portability of identity information across otherwise autonomous security domains. The ultimate goal of identity federation is to enable users of one domain to securely access data or systems of another domain seamlessly, and without the need for completely redundant user administration. Identity federation comes in many flavors, including "user-controlled" or "user-centric" scenarios, as well as enterprise controlled or Business to Business (B2B) scenarios.

Federation is enabled through the use of open industry standards and/or openly published specifications, such that multiple parties can achieve interoperability for common use cases. Typical use-cases involve things such as cross-domain, web-based single sign-on, cross-domain user account provisioning, cross-domain entitlement management and cross-domain user attribute exchange.

4.2.2 Privacy, compliance issues and safeguards in Cloud Computing

Very central to any security and privacy discussion is personal identifiable information (PII). The way this information may be acquired, stored, handled and processed heavily depends on national legislation and regulations. These differences in legislation between the European Union and the USA have for example urged providers to offer within EU territory Cloud data storage solutions in order to be able to sell Cloud services to customers based in Europe. We will first look at a definition of PII, and then at some examples of regulations and legislation.

Personally Identifiable Information (PII)

Let us first look at a definition 'from the Cloud' (Wikipedia):

Personally identifiable information (PII), or Sensitive Personal Information (SPI), as used in US privacy law and information security, is information that can be used on its own or with other information to identify, contact, or locate a single person, or to identify an individual in context. The abbreviation PII is widely accepted in the US context, but the phrase it abbreviates has four common variants based on personal / personally, and identifiable / identifying. Not all are equivalent, and for legal purposes the effective definitions vary depending on the jurisdiction and the purposes for which the term is being used.

(http://en.wikipedia.org/wiki/Personally_identifiable_information as viewed on 18-09-2015))

Examples:

- Types of identification: SSN, passport, fingerprints, iris-scans
- Occupational: job title, company name
- Financial: bank numbers, credit records, PIN-number
- Healthcare: insurance, genetic
- Online activity: log-ins
- Demographic: ethnicity
- Contact: phone, e-mail, social media accounts, address

Some examples of legislation and regulations the use of PII must comply with are:
- USA: the Privacy Act 1974, federal laws HIPAA & GLBA and Safe harbor
- Japan: Personal Information Protection Law and Law for Protection of Computer Processed Data Held by Administrative Organs (2007)
  http://www.cas.go.jp/jp/seisaku/hourei/data/APPIHAO.pdf
- Canada: PIPEDA (Personal Information Protection and Electronic Documents Act, last amended on June 23,2015) and Privacy Act - https://www.priv.gc.ca/leg_c/r_o_p_e.asp
- EU: Laws and privacy standards of the member countries, EU Internet Privacy Law (DIRECTIVE 2002/58/EC, 2002), EU Data Protection Directive (1995), ePrivacy Directive.
  https://ec.europa.eu/digital-agenda/en/online-privacy

> Directive 2002/58/EC of the European Parliament and of the Council of 12 July 2002 and DIRECTIVE 95/46/EC OF THE EUROPEAN PARLIAMENT AND OF THE COUNCIL of 24 October 1995: "personal data". It is defined in the Directive (article 2 a) as follows:
>
> "personal data shall mean any information relating to an identified or identifiable natural person ('data subject'); an identifiable person is one who can be identified, directly or indirectly, in particular by reference to an identification number or to one or more factors specific to his physical, physiological, mental, economic, cultural or social identity."

It is clear that this causes quite a headache for globally operating Cloud providers, basically meaning for virtually every Cloud provider. Customers of Cloud providers will have to check with regular audits if their own compliance is not compromised by using Cloud services.

To summarize, good safeguards need to be put in place in a Cloud environment starting with effective Access Control and Audit; i.e., Single Sign-On (SSO), strong authentication: password & biometric measure and review on audit logs. Secure Cloud Storage requires encryption and Integrity control by mechanisms as hashing. A secure Network Infrastructure uses encryption protocols against leakage and Integrity protocols (digital signatures) against modification. When considering the use of Cloud services from a provider outside your own country or region, it is advisable to consult a lawyer specialized in international legislation regarding security and privacy law.

Exam preparation: chapter 4

'Get it' questions

1. What are the most common security risks in the Cloud?
2. Which measures can be taken to mitigate each security risk?
3. Define what Triple A means in terms of Authentication.
4. Explain the SSO principle.
5. How can PII be used? Give four examples of PII.

Exam Terms

Security, compliance, mitigating measures, Federation, Identity management, privacy, authentication, authorization, accounting (Triple A), Single sign-on (SSO), safeguards and PII.

Evaluation of Cloud Computing: exam specifications

After reading chapter 5 you will understand the principles of Evaluation of Cloud Computing (15%).

5.1 You understand the business case for Cloud Computing (10%)

You can:

5.1.1 Describe the costs and possible savings of Cloud Computing

5.1.2 Describe the main operational and staffing benefits of Cloud Computing

5.2 You understand evaluation of Cloud Computing implementations (5%)

You can:

5.2.1   Describe the evaluation of performance factors, management requirements and satisfaction factors

5.2.2 Describe the evaluation of service providers and their services in Cloud Computing

5. Evaluation of Cloud Computing

5.1 The business case for Cloud Computing

When considering the main business drivers for moving to the Cloud the criteria below will be part of everyone's wish list. However, in which order will depend on the type, size and present IT Infrastructure of an organization. Cloud services provide much more flexibility and better time to market (TTM) of business solutions like new business applications. Top driver for any Chief Financial Officer (CFO) will be price or costs. Going into the Cloud means less Capital Expenditure (CAPEX) in IT infrastructure, and shows immediate results in your ledger.

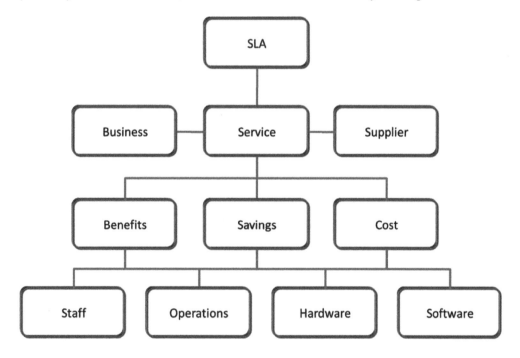

Of course you will want to put your requirements, expectations and key performance indicators in writing, so the next criterion will be Service level agreements (SLAs): performance, security, scalability, availability, support and compliance are among the key ingredients.

For some organizations the type of Cloud architecture and the various building blocks will be of interest. Examples are organizations that want to integrate part of their infrastructure with the provider's infrastructure (does my software stack align with the PaaS service provider's stack?). Or maybe you want to choose a SaaS provider that uses API's that are platform and provider independent; this helps you to prevent a future nasty situation of vendor lock-in.

Yet another business driver, for example for not-for-profit organizations like NGO's, may be 'green computing' (environmentally sustainable computing or IT).

5.1.1 Costs and possible savings of Cloud Computing

The first financial model where savings may be expected is total cost of ownership (TCO). But is this really the case? According to Aggarwal & McCabe "Cloud Computing shifts the TCO discussion" (Aggarwal & McCabe 2009, http://www.netsuite.com/portal/pdf/wp-hurwitztco-study-dynamics.pdf). Customers have to be aware that, in their case, only the distribution of the different components that add up to the TCO may change and in the worst case the long term costs may be even higher.

TCO of Cloud Computing is very much domain- or enterprise-dependent. The benefit you get from using cloud-based platforms, public and private, relates directly to the type of organization you are, and the business processes you support. Other factors should be considered as well, such as existing skills of the staff, existing investment in hardware, software, and facilities, as well as existing laws and regulatory pressures. Running TCO models that don't consider the type of organization, as well as many other factors, are unlikely to result in a true holistic value of this technology.

Everyone is now discovering that the real benefit of Cloud Computing is not the cost savings it can bring, but the fact that IT can react much faster and more effectively to changes in the business. This is where TCO models morph from hard and easy to understand calculations, to grey areas that are difficult to understand and prove.

An example are the capital costs or Capital Expenditures (CAPEX); these will be eliminated to a high extend but in its place come subscriptions and pay-per-use costs. Furthermore, when exchanging your own application servers and application management for a SaaS service, you will probably have to buy-in more expensive external support, e.g., consultancy. In that case CAPEX may only be replaced by even higher Operational Expenditures (OPEX). Every customer will have to calculate the financial benefits for their own situation.

Main components in your calculations will be hardware, software and support. For the financial department these will be further broken down into components like into staff costs, depreciation, utility and maintenance. An example of how to break up costs was published on *dummies.com* by Judith Hurwitz, Robin Bloor, Marcia Kaufman, and Fern Halper. In their article "How to Calculate the Cost of Applications in a Cloud Computing Data Center" they use the term total cost of application ownership (TCAO); or what is the total annual cost of ownership (including hardware support plus some amortization costs).

In this article they present the following list of components:
- Server costs
- Storage costs
- Network costs
- Backup and archive costs
- Disaster recovery costs
- Data center infrastructure costs
- Platform costs
- Software maintenance costs (package software)
- Software maintenance costs (in-house software)
- Help desk support costs
- Operational support personnel costs
- Infrastructure software costs

Maybe cost savings are not your primary driver for moving into the Cloud. For a startup company the Cloud offers other advantages like very low CAPEX in IT infrastructure, and a much shorter implementation time of the infrastructure. Small Internet based businesses can be up and running in a very short time.

5.1.2 Main operational and staffing benefits of Cloud Computing

Some real gains from the Cloud will be on the operational and staffing sides of your organization. Operational tasks like implementation, maintenance and support will be performed by the provider, meaning less staff and less training for your remaining staff.

Operational benefits (examples):
- Managed services
- Self-service (unmanaged services)
- Instant server deployment
- Software licensing without impact on CAPEX
- Uptimes are guaranteed

- Back-ups as a Service (always off-site)

Staffing benefits (examples):
- Less IT staff (less wages to be paid)
- Lower recruitment, HR and training costs
- Lower employee benefits

5.2 Evaluation of Cloud Computing implementations

5.2.1 The evaluation of performance factors, management requirements and satisfaction factors

When it comes to performance you will need to realize that exchanging your own systems and staff for Cloud solutions also means that support and maintenance are no longer in-house, and may take longer to be performed. Furthermore, do you know how well security is organized?

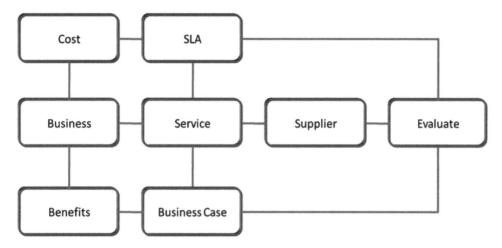

Typical questions to be asked are:
- How long does it take to resolve incidents and problems?
- How robust is the security of the Cloud data center?
- How does system performance (i.e. connection and transaction speeds) compare to your own data center and private network?

It makes sense to do a comparative study of several providers before you sign a contract.

5.2.2 The evaluation of service providers and their services in Cloud Computing

After your survey and due diligence investigations you have signed the contracts with your Cloud provider(s). According to the Service Level Agreements (SLAs) you have a good picture of what is promised, and you can sit down and relax! Or maybe not?

You need to realize that part or most of your key IT processes are now out of your hands. You will need to make sure that you have put a proper governance framework in place. On the performance side this typically means monthly technical performance reports, exception reports and quarterly management reviews.

Additionally, on the compliance side, you will need to make sure that yearly IT audits are performed. Ideally there will be a section in the SLA with this requirement. On a yearly basis you will have to request a: *Statement on Auditing Standards No. 70 (SAS70)*; third-party assurance for service organizations, SSAE 16 (enhancement to the current standard for Reporting on Controls at a Service Organization, the SAS70) and the *International Standards for Assurance Engagements No. 3402 (ISAE3402)*; Assurance Reports on Controls at a Service Organization. If your provider is ISO certified; i.e., ISO/IEC 20000, ISO27001, etc., you will need to ask for a third party statement for those as well.

Exam preparation: chapter 5

'Get it' questions

1. Does Capital Expenditure (CAPEX) in Cloud Computing always result in savings or reduction of costs?

2. What types of benefit are listed below, operational or staffing?

Benefit:	Operational (mark with X)	Staffing (mark with X)
Instant server deployment		
Less training		
Backups as a service		
Managed services		

3. Before you sign a contract with a Cloud provider, it is wise to prepare yourself and to do a comparative study of several providers. Name three typical questions to be asked during preparation.

4. After you have signed the contracts with your Cloud provider, most of the IT processes are out of your hand. You will need to make sure that you have put a proper governance framework in place. What does this mean?

Exam Terms

Evaluation, costs and savings, operational benefits, performance factors, management requirements, satisfaction and evaluation of service providers, Capital Expenditure (CAPEX), Operational Expenditure (OPEX)

6. List of Basic Concepts

Terms are listed in alphabetical order.

Core Concepts

- Application hosting
- Authentication, Authorization, Accounting (AAA, Triple A)
- Availability
- Back-up service
- Capital Expenditure (CAPEX)
- Claim based solution
- Client-Server
- Cloud access architecture
- Cloud Computing
- Cloud presence
- Common Internet File System (CIFS)
- Compliance
- Confidentiality
- Denial-of-service attack (DoS)
- Deployability
- Digital identity
- Distributed Denial-of-service (DDOS)
- Distributed Management Task Force (DMTF)
- Dropbox
- Encrypted federation
- Extensible Markup Language (XML)
- Extensible Messaging and Presence Protocol (XMPP)
- Extranet
- Failover
- Federation
- Guest operating system
- Hybrid Cloud
- Hyper Text Markup Language (HTML)
- Hypervisor
- Identity
- Identity management
- Infrastructure as a Service (IaaS)
- Instant messaging (IM)
- Instant Messaging and Presence Service (IMPS)
- Integrity
- Internet Protocol Security (IPSec)
- Interoperability
- Intranet
- IT infrastructure
- IT service
- JavaScript
- Latency
- Local Area Network (LAN)
- Location independent
- Loosely coupled
- Mainframe
- Man-in-the-middle attack
- Messaging protocol
- Microcomputer
- Middleware
- Migration

- Minicomputer
- Mobile device
- Mobility
- Multimedia Message Service (MMS)
- Multiprocessing
- Multi-programming
- Multiprotocol Label Switching (MPLS)
- Multipurpose architecture
- Multi-sides
- Multi-user
- Network
- Network Attached Storage (NAS)
- Network infrastructure
- Network protocol
- Online games
- Open System Interface (OSI)
- Open Virtualization Format (OVF)
- Open-ID
- Operating system
- Operational benefit
- Operational Expenditure (OPEX)
- Pay-as-you-go model
- Performance factors
- Permissive federation
- Personal Identifiable Information
- Platform as a Service (PaaS)
- Portability
- Privacy
- Privacy notice
- Private Cloud
- Public Cloud
- Recovery
- Redundancy
- Remote datacenter
- Replication
- Risk
- Satisfaction factors
- Scalability
- Scripting language
- Security
- Server
- Service level
- Service Level Agreement (SLA)
- Service Oriented Architecture (SOA)
- Single sign-on (SSO)
- Software as a service (SaaS)
- Staffing benefit
- Stakeholder
- Subcontracted supplier
- Supplier contract
- Supplier management
- Support
- Thin client
- Throughput
- Tiered architecture
- Time to Value
- Time-to-market
- Total Cost of Ownership (TCO)
- Traceability
- Transmission Control Protocol / Internet Protocol (TCP/IP)
- Utility
- Verified federation
- Virtual Machine (VM)
- Virtual Private Network (VPN)
- Virtualization
- Virtualized environment
- Web browser
- Web frontend
- Workload

- **Additional terms**
- Application
- Audit
- Back-up
- Bandwidth
- Bits per second (bps)
- Blog
- Business logic
- Bytes per second (Bps)
- Cell phone
- Client
- Common carrier
- Cost
- Customer
- Customer Relation Management tool
- Data center
- Database
- Datacenter architecture
- E-commerce
- Economic benefit
- E-mail
- Frame relay network
- Green IT
- Hardware
- Institute for Electrical and Electronics Engineers (IEEE)
- International Standards Organization (ISO)
- JavaScript Object Notation (JSON)
- Memory
- National Security Agency (NSA)
- Open Cloud Consortium (OCC)
- Pretty Good Privacy (PGP)
- Processing
- Protocol Analyzer
- Short Message Service (SMS)
- Slide share
- Smartphone
- Social media
- Software
- Storage
- Storage Management Initiative-Specification (SMI-S)
- System Management Architecture for System Hardware (SMASH)
- Track
- User
- Video telecommunication
- Virtualization Management Initiative (VMAN)
- Virus (infection)
- Voice-over-IP (VoIP)
- Web Service Management (WS-MAN)
- Web-based Enterprise Management (WBEM)
- Webmail
- Website
- Wiki
- Wikispace

7. Literature and references

- Aitoro, Jill R. (2008); The Basics: A Glossary of Federal Technology – Identity Management, www.nextgov.com
- Aggarwal, S. & McCabe, L.; The Compelling TCO Case for Cloud Computing in SMB and Mid-Market Enterprises, 2009, Hurwitz & Associates.
- Baker, Jason; How to Evaluate Cloud Computing Providers, By: Industry Perspectives - June 1st, 2010.
- Bernstein, P.A. (1996); Middleware: a model for distributed system services. Commun. ACM 39(2) (1996) 86–98
- Carr, Nicholas; The Big Switch: Rewiring the World, from Edison to Google, W. W. Norton & Company 2008. ISBN 9780393062281.
- Cloud Industry Forum (CIF); Cloud UK - Paper five: Cloud Definitions, Deployment Considerations & Diversity (2012)
- Cloud Security Alliance "The Notorious Nine Cloud Computing Top Threats in 2013, https://downloads.cloudsecurityalliance.org/initiatives/top_threats/
- Encyclopaedia Britannica (Britannica.com, 2015)
- Geva, Perry; Evaluating Cloud computing services: Criteria to consider, http://searchCloudcomputing.techtarget.com/.
- Greene, Tim; Researchers find "massive" security flaws in Cloud architectures, Network World (October 26, 2011).
- Harding, Chris (2011); Cloud Computing For Business, The Open Group Guide, Van Haren Publishing. ISBN: 978 90 8753 657 2
- Hurwitz, Judith - Bloor, Robin - , Kaufman, Marcia and Halper, Fern; How to Calculate the Cost of Applications in a Cloud Computing Data Center (www.dummies.com)
- International Standards Organization (2014);ISO/IEC 17788 Information technology — Cloud computing — Overview and vocabulary, www.iso.org
- Krill, Paul (2009); The Cloud-SOA connection - IT groups that understand SOA may be able to take better advantage of the Cloud, Paul Krill (InfoWorld - February 10, 2009)
- Kuznetzky, Daniel (2011); Virtualization: A Manager's Guide, O'Reilly Media. ISBN-10: 1449306454.
- Lemos, Robert; Recent Breaches Spur New Thinking On Cloud Security, www.darkreading.com (May 02, 2011).

- Livingstone, Rob; How Low Cost Is That Low-Cost Cloud?, The Cloud | September 08, 2011 | CFO.com | US.
- Load balancing is key to successful Cloud-based (dynamic) architectures, (January 23, 2009), www.Devcentral.f5.com
- McKay, Dimitri (2010); Evaluating Cloud Solutions - What Type of Cloud is Right for Me? (December 03, 2010), www.securityweek.com
- NIST Special Publication 800-145 (September 2011)
- Parkhill, Douglas (1966); The Challenge of the Computer Utility, Addison-Wesley. ISBN 0201057204.
- Srinivasan Sundara Rajan (2011); Multi-Tenancy Misconceptions in Cloud Computing (June 15, 2011), Copyright © 2011 SYS-CON Media, Inc.
- Tetz, Edward; Cisco Networking OSI Model Layers (www.dummies.com)
- Woude, M.R. van der (2011); Een heldere kijk op Cloud Computing, Nobel. (www.euroCloud.org)

Organizations

In the main text reference is made to the following not-for-profit organizations and consortia.

Organization	Link / description
Centre4Cloud Dutch Cloud competence centre.	www.centre4Cloud.nl (Dutch language only) Het Centre4Cloud is een nationaal kenniscentrum gericht op open innovatie en de ontwikkeling van kennis rondom Cloud Computing. Het kenniscentrum is een initiatief van Kennispark Twente, Universiteit Twente en Caase.com. Centre4Cloud is mede mogelijk gemaakt door de provincie Overijssel.
EuroCloud EuroCloud is a full European and independant non-profit organization.	http://www.euroCloud.org With EuroCloud presence in 28 countries it is the first Cloud community in Europe. EuroCloud has been involved in addressing the barriers mentioned by VP Kroes as working group leader on Trust, Security and Certification. The mission of EuroCloud is to enhance the Cloud business across Europe between its members and acts as a bridge between local and European Industries, Politics and user organisations. EuroCloud developed as the first association a Cloud certification program, based on existing global standards.
The Cloud Industry Forum (CIF) an industry body that champions and advocates the adoption and use of Cloud-based services by businesses and individuals.	http://www.Cloudindustryforum.org The Cloud Industry Forum was established in 2009 to provide transparency through certification to a Code of Practice for credible online Cloud service providers and to assist end users in determining core information necessary to enable them to adopt these services.

Cloud Security Alliance (CSA) a not-for-profit organization with a mission to promote the use of best practices for providing security assurance within Cloud Computing	www.Cloudsecurityalliance.org The Cloud Security Alliance (CSA) is a not-for-profit organization with a mission to promote the use of best practices for providing security assurance within Cloud Computing, and to provide education on the uses of Cloud Computing to help secure all other forms of computing. The Cloud Security Alliance is led by a broad coalition of industry practitioners, corporations, associations and other key stakeholders.
International Standards Organization (ISO) ISO (International Organization for Standardization) is the world's largest developer and publisher of International Standards.	www.ISO.org ISO is a network of the national standards institutes of 163 countries, one member per country, with a Central Secretariat in Geneva, Switzerland, that coordinates the system. ISO is a non-governmental organization that forms a bridge between the public and private sectors. On the one hand, many of its member institutes are part of the governmental structure of their countries, or are mandated by their government. On the other hand, other members have their roots uniquely in the private sector, having been set up by national partnerships of industry associations.
The National Institute of Standards and Technology's web site (NIST) The National Institute of Standards and Technology (NIST) is an agency of the U.S. Department of Commerce.	http://www.nist.gov Founded in 1901, today, NIST measurements support the smallest of technologies—nanoscale devices so tiny that tens of thousands can fit on the end of a single human hair—to the largest and most complex of human-made creations, from earthquake-resistant skyscrapers to wide-body jetliners to global communication networks.

The Open Group

The Open Group is a global consortium that enables the achievement of business objectives through IT standards.

http://www.opengroup.org/

The mission of The Open Group is to drive the creation of Boundaryless Information Flow™ achieved by:

- Working with customers to capture, understand and address current and emerging requirements, establish policies, and share best practices
- Working with suppliers, consortia and standards bodies to develop consensus and facilitate interoperability, to evolve and integrate specifications and open source technologies
- Offering a comprehensive set of services to enhance the operational efficiency of consortia
- Developing and operating the industry's premier certification service and encouraging procurement of certified products

Answer Key

Chapter 1

'Get it' questions:

1. Private:
   - Resides on a private network that runs on (part of) a data center that is exclusively used by one organization.
   - Owned, managed and run by either the organization itself, a third party or a combination of the two.
   - Support the organization's business objectives in an economic sound way
   - High security (compliance with legislation and regulations).

   Simplistically seen this comprises all forms of private hosting with Internet accessibility.

Public:
   - Delivery of off-site services over the Internet;
   - sharing of resources: 'multi-tenancy' means a potential lower level of security and privacy;
   - aimed at a wide audience;
   - compelling services like E-mail and social media;
   - enables social networking and collaboration.

   Some examples are: Skype, Dropbox, Google Docs, Windows Live, I-Cloud, Hyves and many other Cloud services available to the general public through the Internet. Also (for enterprises) services like Google Apps for business, Windows 365, Service Now (service management), and many more.

Community:
   - A type of shared Private Cloud;
   - delivers services to a specific group of organizations and/or individuals that share a common goal;
   - easy sharing of data, platforms and applications;

- Sharing of capital expenditure for otherwise (too) expensive facilities
- 24/7 access and support;
- shared service and support contracts;
- economics of scale.

Examples: regional or national educational or research institutes, community centers, etc.

Hybrid:

- a mix of the above models; combining several private and public Cloud solutions from several providers into one (virtual) IT infrastructure
- choosing specific services for either Private or Public Cloud suitability is balancing:
  o security
  o privacy
  o compliance versus price

2. Key characteristics SaaS:
   - Software hosted offsite;
   - software on demand;
   - software package;
   - no modification of the software;
   - plug-in software: external software used with internal applications (Hybrid Cloud);
   - vendor with advanced technical knowledge;
   - user entangled with vendor.

Key characteristics PaaS:
   - Mostly used for remote application development;
   - remote application support;
   - platform may have special features;
   - low development costs.

Key characteristics IaaS:
   - Dynamic scaling;
   - desktop virtualization;
   - policy-based services.

3. Key factors:
   - The development of the Internet;
   - the move from Mainframe computing to the present day myriad of personal devices with connection to the Internet;
   - the development of computer networks.

4. To make the Internet accessible to everyone, first there needed to be two other developments, personal devices and network connectivity.

5. Kuznetzky recognizes six different types of virtualization (Kuznetzky, 2011):
   - Access virtualization — Allows access to any application from any device
   - Application virtualization — Enables applications to run on many different operating systems and hardware platforms
   - Processing virtualization — Makes one system seem like many, or many seem like one
   - Network virtualization — Presents an artificial view of the network that differs from the physical reality
   - Storage virtualization — Allows many systems to share the same storage devices, enables concealing the location of storage systems, and more

   Wikipedia mentions seven different types of virtualization:
   - Hardware;
   - desktop;
   - software;
   - memory;
   - storage;
   - data;
   - network.

6. In the past most architectures were proprietary and single purpose. Examples are accounting systems and storage of health care data. This infrastructure had only one purpose. Key to Cloud Computing is that the infrastructure is multipurpose. An example could be a system on which data is not only stored, but also distributed over the Internet.

7. Service-Oriented Architecture (SOA) is an architectural style that supports service orientation. Service orientation is a way of thinking in terms of services and service-based development and the outcomes of services.

8. Drivers:
- Reduced cost
- Automated
- Flexibility
- More Mobility
- Shared Resources
- Agility and scalability
- Back to core business
- More IT functionality for lower price

Limitations:
- Internet access
- Security
- Privacy
- Service level agreement
- Vendor lock-in

Chapter 2

'Get it' questions:

1. Main hardware and main software components have to be part of the local Cloud environment.

2. The key benefits of using a VPN are:
   - Remote secure connectivity; extends your LAN/WAN to a global scale.
   - Cheaper than using traditional rented network connections; it makes use of standard Internet connections through DSL connections at home or fast cellphone network data connections.
   - More mobility for employees; improve productivity for employees working from their home

3. Some of the available options are having a wall between data from different clients, zoning, hidden storage and role based customer and user profiles (this means anonymity, you do not know who your neighbors are).

4. Process groups and processes:

Process group	Process
Service delivery processes	Service level management
	Service reporting
	Service continuity and availability management
	Budgeting and accounting for IT Services
	Capacity management
	Information security management
Relationship processes	Business relationship management
	Supplier management
Control processes	Configuration management
	Change management
Resolution processes	Incident management
	Problem management
Release process	Release management

Chapter 3

1. Basic ingredients:
   - "any" web enabled device
   - PC, laptop, tablet, smart phone, thin client
   - Internet browser
   - Internet connection
   - Provider, IP-address
   - Cloud based application
   - SaaS solution

2. The use of standard protocol and other design standards, and virtualization.

3. A Thin Client is a simple network enabled computer without a hard disk (it boots from the network) or any other moving parts (no DVC drive).
   Benefits:
   - Lower costs; initial price and running costs
   - Simple; no moving parts
   - Better for the environment; they produce less heat and need less cooling, sometimes not even a fan
   - Heightened security; booting from the network with controlled access, no local data, etc.
   - Less chance of user errors

4.

Category	Target audience	Examples
Customer Relationship Management (CRM)	Large corporations, public sector organizations or NGO's	Salesforce.com, SugarCRM, NetSuite
Enterprise Resource Planning (ERP)	Large corporations, public sector organizations or NGO's	NetSuite, Compiere (open source), Microsoft Dynamics AX ERP
HR solutions	Large corporations, public sector organizations or NGO's Small enterprises	Taleo, FinancialForce.com Human Capital Management (HCM) Natural HR
IT Service Management	Large corporations, public sector organizations or NGO's	ServiceNow
Finance & accounting	Large corporations, public sector organizations or NGO's	Intacct, NetSuite
Office suites	Large and small enterprises	Microsoft Office 365, Google Apps for Work, Zoho Office Suite
Video conferencing	SMEs/SMBs	Skype, WebEx Meeting Center

5. The relationship between provider and customer changes:
   - Customer intimacy: running the customer's business
   - Running the whole supply chain

6. Benefits: business opportunities
   - New lease of life for "old" data centers (IaaS)
   - Better use of resources because of multi-tenancy
   - Economics of scale
   - Quickly develop and run applications in the same environment (PaaS)

Risks: challenges

- Compliance
- Standards, legislation and regulations
- Performance
- Availability, capacity, flexibility, scalability
- Security
- Privacy

Chapter 4

'Get it' questions:

1. The most common security risks are:
   - Data loss/leakage
   - Shared technology vulnerabilities
   - Insecure application interfaces
   - Malicious insiders
   - Abuse and nefarious use of Cloud Computing
   - Unknown risk profile and account
   - Account, service and traffic hijacking

2. Measures to take:

   Data loss/leakage

   Examples of mitigating measures that can be taken are authentication, audit (i.e. ISO/IEC 27001, Data Security) and authorization, as well as use of encryption and a proper backup strategy.

   Shared technology vulnerabilities

   Examples of mitigating measures that can be taken are enhanced operations procedures for monitoring and escalations when security breaches and application of good security practice for installation, configuration and application of patches.

   Insecure application interfaces

   Examples of mitigating measures that can be taken are designing for security, proper testing methods, understanding how they interact with other interfaces and software and strong authentication and access control.

   Malicious insiders

   Examples of mitigating measures that can be taken are good HR vetting procedures, strong information security policies and procedures.

   Abuse and nefarious use of Cloud Computing

   Examples of mitigating measures that can be taken are validation of credentials, increased monitoring of traffic between customers and known suspicious sites.

Unknown risk profile and account

Examples of mitigating measures that can be taken are good SLA structures including Cloud provider compliance audits.

Account, service and traffic hijacking

Examples of mitigating measures that can be taken are strong authentication techniques and monitoring of user behavior.

3. Triple-A, often named AAA means authentication, authorization, and accounting. These elements are the security corner stones of IP based network management and policy administration.

4. One of the authentication challenges is formed by the fact that Cloud (i.e. web) based security infrastructure is distributed. Security features and algorithms are spread all over a certain domain. A solution for this problem is offered by the Single Sign On (SSO) principle. All distributed security elements are consolidated on one SSO-server. As a result, a user only needs to sign on once using a security measure like a smart-card, a security token or an active directory (AD) account. SSO architecture uses the so-called SOAP protocol, a protocol for the exchange of information in the implementation of Web Services in the Cloud or any other network.

5. Personally Identifiable Information (PII) is information that can be used to uniquely identify, contact, or locate a single person or can be used with other sources to uniquely identify a single individual.

Examples:
- Types of identification: SSN, passport, fingerprints, iris-scans
- Occupational: job title, company name
- Financial: bank numbers, credit records, PIN-number
- Health care: insurance, genetic
- Online activity: log-ins
- Demographic: ethnicity
- Contact: phone, e-mail, social media accounts, address

Chapter 5

'Get it' questions:

1. Capital expenditure will be eliminated to a high extend but in its place come subscriptions and pay-per-use costs. Furthermore, when exchanging your own application servers and application management for a SaaS service, you will probably have to buy-in more expensive external support (i.e. consultancy). In that case capital expenditures (CAPEX) may only be replaced by even higher Operational Expenditures (OPEX). Every customer will have to calculate the financial benefits for his own situation.

2. Operational benefits (examples):
   - Managed services
   - Self-service (unmanaged services)
   - instant server deployment
   - software licensing without impact on Capex
   - uptimes are guaranteed
   - Backups as a service (always off-site)

   Staffing benefits (examples):
   - Less IT staff (less wages to be paid)
   - Lower recruitment, HR and training costs
   - Lower employee benefits

3. Typical questions to be asked are:
   - How long does it take to resolve incidents and problems?
   - How robust is the security of the Cloud data center?
   - How does system performance (i.e. connection and transaction speeds) compare to your own data center and private network?

4. On the performance side this typically means monthly technical performance reports, exception reports and quarterly management reviews. Additionally, on the compliance side, you will need to make sure that yearly IT or EDP audits are performed.

Contact EXIN

www.exin.com